Gooseberry Patch

A Country Store In Your Mailbox®

W9-CEF-743

Magic of Christmas

Melt-in-your-mouth recipes, memories
of winter fun & handmade gifts that
bring holiday cheer!

A Country Store In Your Mailbox®

Gooseberry Patch
149 Johnson Drive
Department BOOK
Delaware, OH 43015
★
1-800·854·6673
gooseberrypatch.com

Copyright 2001, Gooseberry Patch 1-888052-82-1
First Printing, April, 2001

How To Subscribe

Would you like to receive
"A Country Store in Your Mailbox"®?
For a 2-year subscription to our 96-page
Gooseberry Patch catalog, simply send $3.00 to:

Gooseberry Patch
P.O. Box 190
Department BOOK
Delaware, OH 43015

Contents

Dedication

For everyone who loves
rosy cheeks, making snow angels
and creamy cocoa!

Appreciation

THANK you for making
this Christmas
our most magical yet!

Cookies & Candy

Yummy homemade treats to start the Season.

Oatmeal-Caramel Bars

Merrie Ellen O'Donnell
Security, CO

Caramel, nuts and chocolate...these are simply delicious!

1 c. plus 3 T. all-purpose flour,
    divided
1 c. long-cooking oats,
    uncooked
3/4 c. brown sugar, packed
1/2 t. baking soda

1/4 t. salt
3/4 c. butter, melted
1 c. chocolate chips
1/2 c. chopped nuts
3/4 c. caramel ice cream topping

In a large mixing bowl, combine one cup flour, oats, brown sugar, baking soda, salt and butter. Press half of the mixture into a greased 13"x9" baking dish. Bake at 350 degrees for 10 minutes, then sprinkle chocolate chips and nuts over top. In a small mixing bowl, combine caramel topping and remaining flour; stirring until well blended. Drizzle mixture over chocolate chips and nuts, sprinkle remaining brown sugar mixture on top. Bake an additional 15 to 20 minutes. Cut in bars. Makes 12 to 14 servings.

Turn cookies into yummy edible place markers...just use frosting to add each guest's name!

Cookies & Candy

Peanut Butter Creme Candy

Nancy Wilkins
Gastonia, NC

So simple, you don't even have to measure the ingredients for this recipe...they can all be bought in the right size containers.

1-lb. pkg. powdered sugar
5-oz. can evaporated milk

12-oz. jar creamy peanut butter
7-oz. jar marshmallow creme

In a large saucepan, combine powdered sugar and milk; cook over medium heat until candy thermometer reaches 240 degrees or firm ball stage; stir constantly. Remove from heat, blend in peanut butter and marshmallow creme. Pour into a greased 13"x9" baking dish, chill until set and cut into squares. Makes 1-1/2 pounds.

Almond Toffee Popcorn

Erin Jones
Smyer, TX

Crunchy and sweet...irresistible for munching on.

1 c. sugar
1/2 c. butter
1/2 c. corn syrup
1/4 c. water

1 c. chopped almonds, toasted
1/2 t. vanilla extract
1/2 c. popcorn, popped

In a large saucepan, combine sugar, butter, corn syrup, water and almonds. Cook over medium heat until candy thermometer reaches 280 degrees on a candy thermometer or soft crack stage. Add vanilla; stir well. Place popcorn in a large mixing bowl; coat with sugar mixture. Makes about 2 cups.

7

Creamy Almond Mints

Hattie Douthit
Crawford, NE

If you don't have molds, just drop by teaspoonfuls on wax paper.

8-oz. pkg. cream cheese,
   softened
paste food coloring

1-1/2 t. almond extract
1-lb. pkg. powdered sugar
1/2 c. sugar

Combine cream cheese with enough paste food coloring to get the desired color; blend in almond extract. Add enough powdered sugar to form a soft dough that isn't sticky. Roll mixture in walnut-size balls, coat with sugar and press into your favorite molds. Remove and let dry thoroughly. Makes about one pound.

Sugar Plum Pecans

Karen Norman
Jacksonville, FL

*Great for snacking on...make some to enjoy while watching
your favorite holiday movie.*

1-1/2 c. sugar
1/2 c. water
1/4 c. corn syrup

1/2 t. vanilla extract
2 c. whole pecans

Combine sugar, water and corn syrup in a medium saucepan. Bring to a boil and continue to boil until candy thermometer reaches 240 degrees on a candy thermometer; remove from heat. Add vanilla and pecans, stirring until thick, creamy and white. Working quickly at room temperature, pour onto wax paper and separate with fingers. Makes 2 cups.

Shop flea markets and tag sales for vintage candy molds in Santa, reindeer and snowman shapes...they really add whimsey to a holiday kitchen!

Cookies & Candy

Ultimate Oatmeal Cookies

Michael Mulhern
Windham, OH

"Awesome" is the only word to describe these cookies!

2-1/2 sticks butter, softened
1/2 c. sugar
1-1/2 c. brown sugar, packed
1-1/2 t. vanilla extract
1-1/2 t. cinnamon
1/2 t. nutmeg
1/2 t. salt
4 T. honey
1 t. baking soda

3 eggs
2 c. whole-wheat flour
3 c. quick-cooking oats,
  uncooked
1/2 c. raisins
1/4 c. dried cranberries
1/2 c. white chocolate chips
1/4 c. chopped pecans
1/4 c. chopped macadamia nuts

Cream together butter and sugars; add vanilla, cinnamon, nutmeg, salt, honey, baking soda and eggs. Beat until smooth and thoroughly combined. Blend in flour, oats, raisins, cranberries, chocolate chips and nuts. Drop by tablespoonfuls on an ungreased baking sheet. Bake at 350 degrees for 12 to 14 minutes or until golden. Makes about 2-1/2 dozen.

What's your favorite treat to leave Santa and why?
"Cheese and milk because the cheese is cheesy and he likes it."

Kyle & Sean, ages 6 and 3

Sweet & Sticky S'more Bars

Jo Ann

A favorite campfire treat in a bar cookie!

2 c. graham cracker crumbs
1/3 c. sugar
1/4 t. salt

1/2 c. butter, melted
16 oz. semi-sweet chocolate
4 c. mini marshmallows

Blend together first 4 ingredients; set aside one cup. Press remaining mixture in an ungreased 13"x9" baking dish and bake at 350 degrees for 10 minutes, or until golden; let cool. Melt chocolate in a double boiler and spread over cooled crust. Layer on marshmallows, pressing gently into warm chocolate; top with one cup reserved graham cracker mixture. Broil 2 inches from heat source until marshmallows are lightly golden; cool and cut in squares. Makes 1-1/2 dozen.

Count down the 12 Days of Christmas!
Bake and decorate 12 different cookies, then slip each
one in a clear envelope to enjoy each day.

Cookies & Candy

Candy Cane Cookies

Amie Underwood
McCool Junction, NE

So pretty...leave some out for Santa!

1/2 c. sugar
1/4 c. margarine
1 egg
1 T. milk
1 c. all-purpose flour

1/2 t. baking powder
1/4 t. salt
1/4 t. baking soda
1/4 c. peppermint candy,
   crushed

Cream together sugar and margarine, beat in egg and milk; set aside. Combine flour, baking powder, salt and baking soda; add to sugar mixture. Fold in peppermint candy and stir gently. Drop dough by teaspoonfuls onto a greased baking sheet. Bake at 350 degrees for 10 to 12 minutes. Makes about 2 dozen.

Peanut Butter Brownies

Patti Watson
Telford, PA

Doesn't everyone love chocolate and peanut butter?

1 c. butter
3/4 c. brown sugar, packed
2-1/4 c. sugar
5 eggs
15-oz. jar peanut butter

3 c. all-purpose flour
1 t. salt
3 t. baking powder
1 T. vanilla extract
12-oz. tub chocolate frosting

Blend all ingredients together, except frosting, and spoon in a greased 18"x14" pan. Bake at 350 degrees for 20 minutes; don't overbake. Frost while brownies are still hot. Makes about 3 dozen.

THE best of all gifts around any Christmas tree: The presence of a happy family all wrapped up in each other.

-Burton Hillis

Grandma's Peanut Butter Fudge

Cheri Creed
Aberdeen, NC

Rich and very peanutty!

2/3 c. milk
2 c. brown sugar, packed

1/2 c. creamy peanut butter

Heat milk and brown sugar together over medium heat until a candy thermometer reaches 234 degrees. Remove from heat and stir in peanut butter. Pour into a greased 8"x8" baking dish and chill until firm, cut in squares. Makes one pound.

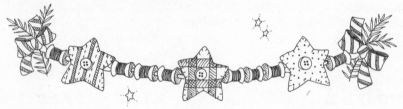

Christmas Wreaths

Roxanne Bixby
West Franklin, NH

The next time your kids enjoy a "snow day", spend part of it making these quick & easy cookies.

30 marshmallows
1/2 c. margarine
1 t. vanilla extract

2 t. green food coloring
3-1/2 c. corn flake cereal
Garnish: maraschino cherries

Heat marshmallows, margarine, vanilla and food coloring in a double boiler until marshmallows melt. Spread corn flake cereal on a baking sheet and carefully pour marshmallow mixture over cereal. Blend well and as mixture cools, form in wreath shapes. Add whole or sliced cherries on top to resemble holly berries. Makes about 2 dozen.

Cookies & Candy

Caramel Corn

Claudia Coffin
Columbia, MO

A favorite we all remember from childhood.

16 c. popcorn, popped
1/2 c. butter
1 c. brown sugar, packed
1/4 c. corn syrup

1-1/2 t. molasses
1/2 t. salt
1 t. vanilla extract
1/4 t. baking soda

Place popcorn in a large metal serving bowl; set aside. In a large saucepan, mix together butter, brown sugar, corn syrup, molasses and salt. Heat to boiling and boil for 5 minutes, stirring constantly. Remove from heat, add vanilla and baking soda; mix well. Pour over popcorn and stir to coat evenly. Place on an ungreased baking sheet. Bake at 250 degrees for one hour, stirring several times. Cool on wax paper for 15 minutes and break into small pieces. Cool completely and store in an airtight container. Makes 16 cups.

Try using half-and-half instead of milk, and adding just a little lemon juice when making powdered sugar icing...really yummy on sugar cookies!

Oatmeal Cookie Cakes

Colleen Haseltine
Marietta, GA

An oatmeal sandwich cookie with a smooth, creamy filling.

2 c. butter
2 c. brown sugar, packed
2 c. sugar
2 t. vanilla
4 eggs
3 c. all-purpose flour

2 t. baking soda
2 t. salt
6 c. quick-cooking oats,
    uncooked
2 c. flaked coconut

Cream together butter, sugars and vanilla. Add eggs, one at a time; set aside. Sift together flour, baking soda and salt; add to butter mixture. Stir in oats and coconut. Drop by teaspoonfuls on a greased baking sheet and bake at 350 degrees for 8 to 10 minutes. Let cool before filling. Makes approximately 8 to 10 dozen.

Filling:

1 c. milk
5 T. all-purpose flour
1/2 c. shortening

1/2 c. margarine
1 c. plus 2 T. sugar
1 t. vanilla extract

Combine milk and flour over medium heat until mixture forms a paste. Cool completely. Add shortening and margarine; stir in sugar and vanilla extract. Spoon between 2 cookies; store in an airtight container in the refrigerator.

Cookies & Candy

Holiday Nut Squares

Nancy Rubeck
Raymond, OH

*These creamy, crunchy squares have been a favorite
at our home for many years.*

3 c. salted peanuts, divided
3 T. butter
2 c. peanut butter chips

14-oz. can sweetened condensed
milk
2 c. mini marshmallows

Place half of the peanuts into an ungreased 11"x7" baking dish; set
aside. In a medium saucepan, melt butter and peanut butter chips over
low heat. Add milk and marshmallows; heat and stir until melted.
Pour over peanuts and sprinkle reserved peanuts on top; cover and
chill. Cut in squares. Makes 5 to 6 dozen.

This year, give neighbors a cookie kit. Fill a basket or
holiday tin with ready-made dough, sprinkles, cookie
cutters, icing and a favorite recipe...they'll love it!

Magical Sugar Cookies

Judith Hertenlehner
Port Charlotte, FL

*Leave out the vanilla and substitute 1/2 teaspoon lemon extract
and 2 teaspoons lemon zest for a yummy variation.*

4 c. all-purpose flour	3 eggs
1/2 t. salt	1 t. vanilla extract
2 c. sugar	1 t. baking soda
1 c. butter-flavored shortening	1 T. hot water

Combine flour, salt and sugar; cut in shortening until coarse crumbs form. Add eggs and vanilla; mix well. In a measuring cup, dissolve baking soda in hot water; add to flour mixture. Knead lightly, then roll to 1/2-inch thickness and cut with your favorite cookie cutter. Place on an ungreased baking sheet and bake at 350 degrees for 10 minutes; do not let brown. Cool and frost. Depending on the size of your cookie cutter, makes approximately 4 to 5 dozen.

Frosting:

3/4 c. powdered sugar	1/2 t. vanilla extract
1 T. butter, melted	1/2 t. lemon juice
1 T. milk	

Blend together all ingredients until smooth. Makes 1/3 cup frosting.

16

Cookies & Candy

Snowballs

Betty Dhority
Moravia, IA

So simple...no baking!

1 c. butter
1/2 c. creamy peanut butter
1-lb. pkg. plus 3/4 c. powdered
   sugar, divided
1 c. flaked coconut

1 c. mini chocolate chips
2 c. quick-cooking oats,
   uncooked
1/2 t. vanilla extract

Combine butter, peanut butter, one pound powdered sugar, coconut, chocolate chips, oats and vanilla extract. Shape mixture into walnut-size balls; roll in remaining powdered sugar. Store in refrigerator. Makes 4 to 5 dozen.

There's no better time than now to make snowmen cookies! Bake the kids' favorite sugar cookies and top with white frosting. Add a chocolate chip smile, raisin eyes and a candy corn nose...how sweet!

Marshmallow Fudge

Barbara Walker
Farmington, MI

A good, old-fashioned fudge...smooth and chocolatey.

3 c. sugar
1 c. evaporated milk
6 T. butter

7-oz. jar marshmallow creme
12-oz. pkg. chocolate chips

In a large saucepan, mix together sugar, milk and butter over medium heat until mixture reaches 234 degrees on a candy thermometer. Remove from heat and add remaining ingredients. Stir until chips are melted. Spread into a greased 9"x9" baking dish. Makes approximately 2 dozen squares.

Christmas! The very word brings joy to our hearts...there is still that same warm feeling we had as children, the same warmth that enfolds our hearts and our homes.

-Joan Winmill Brown

18

Cookies & Candy

Shortbread Cookies

Janet Vaughn
Darien, IL

Nice and crumbly, just as shortbread should be.

1/2 c. butter, softened
1/2 c. margarine, softened
3/4 c. powdered sugar

3/4 c. cornstarch
1-1/2 c. all-purpose flour
Garnish: colored sugar

Cream together butter and margarine; add sugar and mix. Blend in cornstarch, mixing well, and gradually add flour; dough will be very crumbly. Press mixture into an ungreased 15"x11" baking sheet. Sprinkle with colored sugar and bake at 300 degrees for 40 minutes or until golden. While hot, cut in one-inch squares. Makes about 12 dozen.

Dip the edges of your shortbread cookies in melted chocolate, then roll in nuts, colorful sprinkles or crushed peppermint candies...Santa will love 'em!

19

Vanilla Sticks

Bev Shealy
Tiro, OH

My grandmother made these each year at Christmas. They're still everyone's favorite cookie and always disappear fast.

8 egg whites, room temperature   1 T. vanilla extract
2 1-lb. pkgs. powdered sugar   4 to 5 c. almonds, finely ground

In a large mixing bowl, beat egg whites until stiff but not dry. Gradually, add sugar and vanilla. Beat with an electric mixer on medium speed for 15 minutes; divide egg white mixture in half. Add almonds to one half and chill 15 minutes. Set aside remaining half. On a lightly floured piece of wax paper, roll almond mixture to 1/8-inch thick. Spread remaining egg white mixture over almond mixture and cut in 4-1/2 inch strips. Place strips close together on a well greased baking sheet. Let dry for 5 minutes, then bake at 300 degrees for 15 minutes or until golden. Remove immediately from baking sheets. Makes 6 to 7 dozen.

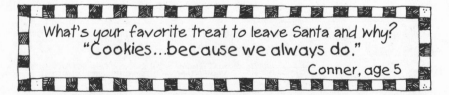

What's your favorite treat to leave Santa and why?
"Cookies...because we always do."

Conner, age 5

Cookies & Candy

Moravian Molasses Cookies

Kitty Berry
Yorktown, VA

A wonderful recipe from Old Salem, a Moravian settlement in North Carolina. These cookies will take quite a bit of time to make, but the results are worth the effort. And yes, you really do get almost 500 cookies!

1 pt. molasses
1/2 lb. brown sugar
1/2 c. shortening
1/2 c. butter
2 T. cinnamon
1 T. ground cloves

1 t. ground ginger
1/4 c. grape juice
1 t. baking soda
1/8 t. salt
7-1/2 to 8-1/2 c. all-purpose flour

Blend together first 10 ingredients; gradually add flour to make a stiff dough. Cover and refrigerate dough at least 24 hours. Divide dough into several portions, rolling each as thin as possible. Cut with your favorite cookie cutters and place on a baking sheet coated with non-stick vegetable spray. Bake at 325 degrees for 12 minutes. Makes approximately 40 dozen.

There are 3 towns in the United States officially named Santa Claus!

Brown Sugar Caramels

Stacie Barth
Salt Lake City, UT

*Old-fashioned, chewy caramels. Wrap up a batch in wax paper
and tuck in painted Shaker boxes for gift-giving.*

1 c. butter, melted
2-1/4 c. brown sugar, packed
1/8 t. salt
1 c. corn syrup

15-oz. can sweetened condensed
    milk
1 t. vanilla extract

In a large saucepan, blend together butter, brown sugar and salt. Stir
in corn syrup and mix well. Gradually add milk, stirring constantly.
Continue to cook and stir over medium heat for 12 to 15 minutes or
until candy thermometer reaches the firm ball stage, 245 degrees.
Remove from heat and add vanilla. Pour into a greased 9"x9" pan.
Cool and cut into squares. Wrap each piece in plastic or wax paper
and store in an airtight container in a cool place. Makes about
1-1/2 pounds.

A cheery snowman potholder makes holiday baking fun!
Use fabric paint on a white potholder to give him eyes,
nose and a mouth...so jolly!

Cookies & Candy

Coffee Crunch Bars

Ann Arbour
Augusta, ME

I always enjoy the potlucks we have at work, but somehow, when the sign up list gets to me, it already has these chocolatey bars next to my name! Sometimes my friends even meet me at the door waiting for them...there are never any leftovers to bring back home.

2 c. brown sugar, packed
2 eggs
1 c. oil
1 c. warm coffee
1 t. vanilla extract

3 c. all-purpose flour
1 t. baking soda
1 t. salt
12-oz. pkg. chocolate chips
11-1/2 oz. can salted peanuts

Combine all ingredients, except chocolate chips and peanuts. Pour mixture in an ungreased 13"x9" baking dish. Top with chocolate chips and peanuts and bake at 350 degrees for 30 minutes. Makes 2 dozen.

How do Santa & Mrs. Claus decorate their home?
"With paintbrushes."

Jack, age 3

Spicy Drop Cookies

Shirley Rupp
Ephrata, PA

Mom always made these fruit-filled cookies as the first cookie of the holiday season. The flavor really does improve the longer they sit...if you can wait to eat them!

2 eggs
1/2 c. shortening
1-1/2 c. brown sugar, packed
2-1/2 c. all-purpose flour
1 t. baking soda
3 T. milk
1/4 t. ground cloves

1/2 t. cinnamon
1/4 t. nutmeg
1 c. raisins
1 c. dried currants
zest of one orange
1/2 c. black walnuts, ground

Cream eggs, shortening and brown sugar until light and fluffy. In a separate, large mixing bowl, combine flour and baking soda; add creamed mixture alternately with milk; blend well. Blend in remaining ingredients and mix well. Drop by teaspoonfuls onto a greased baking sheet. Bake at 350 degrees for 10 to 12 minutes or until cookies puff up and are golden. Makes 2 to 3 dozen.

I stopped believing in Santa Claus when I was 6. Mother took me to see him in a department store and he asked for my autograph.

-Shirley Temple

Cookies & Candy

Holiday Truffles

Liz Plotnick-Snay
Gooseberry Patch

These melt-in-your-mouth candies are incredibly easy to prepare and if you don't like coconut, roll them in ground nuts or cocoa.

2 c. semi-sweet chocolate chips   12-oz. tub chocolate frosting
1 t. orange extract   1 c. flaked coconut

Place chocolate chips in a double boiler and melt over medium heat. Remove from heat and stir in orange extract and frosting; blend well. Refrigerate until firm, about 2 hours. Place coconut in a medium mixing bowl; set aside. Spoon chocolate in one inch balls, mixture will be very sticky. Toss in coconut to coat and place in paper or foil candy cups. Repeat with remaining chocolate. Makes approximately 6 dozen.

Get everyone in their jammies and snuggle up together to read a Christmas book...what a great way to end the day.

25

Coconut Joys

Flo Burtnett
Gage, OK

My daughter and I love these...we can't get enough of them!

1/2 c. margarine
2 c. powdered sugar
3 c. flaked coconut

2 1-oz. squares milk chocolate,
   melted
Garnish: chopped nuts, optional

In a medium saucepan, melt margarine; remove from heat. Add powdered sugar and coconut; mix well. Shape rounded teaspoonfuls into balls. Place balls on a parchment lined baking sheet, then make indentations in the center of each. Fill indentations on each ball with chocolate, sprinkle nuts over chocolate, if desired. Chill 3 hours or until firm. Makes 3 dozen.

Package holiday treats...fudge, peanut brittle, cookies or brownies, in airtight containers, then slip them in gift bags tied with raffia. Set several in a basket by the door so there will always be a treat waiting for guests to take home.

Cookies & Candy

Easy Amaretti

Rosemary Scarpelli
Sterling Heights, MI

Enjoy these the way we do...with a cup of steamy espresso.

4 c. almonds, finely chopped
3 eggs
2 c. sugar
1 T. lemon zest

1 T. almond extract
2 c. powdered sugar
36 whole almonds

Blend together chopped almonds, eggs, sugar, lemon zest and almond extract. Roll teaspoonfuls of dough into walnut-size balls, then roll in powdered sugar. Place each ball on a baking sheet lined with aluminum foil. Place an almond in the center of each ball; pressing down slightly. Bake at 350 degrees for 15 minutes. Makes about 3 dozen.

Don't have a cookie press? Improvise! Lots of glasses have pretty designs on the bottom...just dip in sugar and press on walnut-size balls of dough.

27

Chewy Chocolate Rolls

Kathy Langston
Bell, FL

My fondest memory is making these with my first grade class...they couldn't believe they could make candy! Now, ten years later, when I see their parents, they tell me their kids still make these.

2 T. margarine, softened
1/2 c. corn syrup
2 1-oz. squares unsweetened
    chocolate, melted

1 t. vanilla extract
3 c. powdered sugar
3/4 c. powdered milk

Place all ingredients in a gallon size plastic zipping bag. As you seal the bag securely, remove as much air as possible. Gently squeeze bag to blend ingredients. Remove dough and shape in balls or roll in a rope and cut into one-inch pieces. Makes 1-1/2 pounds.

Make holiday cookies and candy look magical. Sprinkle on edible glitter, confetti and colorful sugar...beautiful.

Cookies & Candy

Candied Popcorn

Judy Kelly
St. Charles, MO

If you love white chocolate and popcorn, this is for you.

8 c. popcorn, popped
3 c. corn puff cereal

2 c. corn chips, slightly crushed
16 oz. white chocolate

In a large mixing bowl, toss together popcorn, cereal and corn chips. Melt chocolate in a double boiler and carefully pour over popcorn mixture; toss to coat evenly. Spread on wax paper for 3 to 4 hours to dry. Makes about 13 cups.

'Twas the night before Christmas, when all through the house, not a creature was stirring, not even a mouse.

–Clement C. Moore

Chocolate Chip Chompers

Monica Roth
Elkhart, IN

*A tin filled with these cookies would be an irresistible treat
for the snacker on your gift list!*

1/2 c. butter
1/2 c. shortening
1 c. brown sugar, packed
1 c. sugar
2 eggs
2 T. hot water

2 t. vanilla extract
3 c. all-purpose flour
1 t. salt
1 t. baking soda
12-oz. pkg. chocolate chips

Cream butter, shortening, brown sugar and sugar together. Add eggs, water and vanilla; beat until fluffy. Whisk together flour, salt and baking soda, stir in chocolate chips and add to brown sugar mixture. Drop by tablespoonfuls onto an ungreased baking sheet. Bake at 375 degrees for 10 to 12 minutes. Let cool for 5 minutes before removing from pan. Makes approximately 3 dozen.

Make several different cookies from just one recipe!
When making a favorite chocolate chip cookie dough,
substitute cinnamon, raspberry, peanut butter or mint
chocolate chips for a new twist.

Cookies & Candy

Old-Fashioned Butter Cookies

Geraldine Sherwood
Schererville, IN

Anyone would be thrilled to receive a basket filled with these irresistible cookies.

3 c. all-purpose flour
1 t. baking powder
1/2 t. salt
1 c. butter

3/4 c. sugar
1 egg
2 T. milk
1-1/2 t. vanilla extract

Thoroughly blend flour, baking powder and salt; set aside. In a separate mixing bowl, cream together butter and sugar. Stir in egg, milk and vanilla. Add dry ingredients gradually to butter mixture and mix well. Chill one hour. Divide dough into 3 sections. Roll first section out on a floured surface to 1/4-inch thickness; cut with cookie cutter. Place on an ungreased baking sheet and bake at 400 degrees for 5 to 8 minutes or until lightly golden. Repeat with remaining dough, then frost. Makes about 3 dozen.

Frosting:

2 T. butter
1/2 t. vanilla extract

1-3/4 c. powdered sugar
4 T. milk

Prepare frosting by creaming butter, vanilla and powdered sugar together. Add milk and beat until light and fluffy. Frost each cookie and store in an airtight container. Makes about one cup.

Holly & Yule Cookies

Kim McGeorge
Ashley, OH

These are so easy and fun for the kids to make. I also like to take them to holiday cookie exchanges…they're so festive!

6 T. margarine
24 marshmallows
1/2 t. vanilla extract
green food coloring

2-1/2 c. corn flake cereal
Garnish: 9-oz. pkg. red
    cinnamon candies

Combine margarine, marshmallows and vanilla in a double boiler. Add green food coloring, a drop at a time, until you get the shade of green you'd like. When mixture is melted and well blended, pour over corn flake cereal; stirring well to coat. Drop by teaspoonfuls on wax paper. Garnish each with cinnamon candies to resemble holly berries. Makes approximately 1-1/2 dozen.

Keep your eyes open year 'round at tag sales and flea markets for anything you might be able to tuck your holiday sweets in...vintage pie tins, mugs, jelly jars or enamelware pails would all be terrific.

Cookies & Candy

Jolly Chocolate Cookies

Margaret Scoresby
Mount Vernon, OH

Sometimes I add chocolate chips for a really chocolatey cookie.

1/2 c. shortening	2 c. all-purpose flour
1-2/3 c. sugar	2 t. baking powder
2 eggs	1/2 t. salt
2 t. vanilla extract	1/3 c. milk
5 T. baking cocoa	1/2 c. chopped nuts

Cream together shortening and sugar; add eggs and vanilla. Blend in cocoa and stir well. Whisk together flour, baking powder and salt. Add flour mixture and milk alternately to cocoa mixture until blended: add nuts. Drop by tablespoonfuls on an ungreased baking sheet. Bake at 350 degrees for 8 to 10 minutes. Makes 4 to 5 dozen.

Animal crackers and cocoa to drink,
that is the finest of suppers, I think;
when I am grown up and can have what I please
I think I shall always insist upon these.

–Christopher Morley

Sending Sweet Treats

If you're sending sweet treats to someone far away, keep these handy tips in mind...

Some cookies ship better than others...choose ones that don't break easily such as, chocolate chip, oatmeal-raisin, snickerdoodles, macaroons, brownies, no-bake and peanut butter.

Pack cookies in separate airtight containers and don't pack crisp cookies with soft ones or you'll find the crisp ones will be soft and the soft ones crisp!

Pack round cookies back-to-back and wrap in wax paper, brownies or really moist cookies should be covered in plastic wrap so they stay chewy.

Tuck the containers in a box and surround them with crumpled newspaper or bubble wrap to cushion them for the journey.

Just for fun, send along a container of frosting, sprinkles, jimmies, edible glitter and sparkly sugar...brownies and sugar cookies can be decorated after they arrive!

Tree-trimming Treats

Tasty tidbits to enjoy while trimming the tree.

Santa's Snack Mix

Laurie Michael
Colorado Springs, CO

As far back as I can remember we've enjoyed this crunchy snack mix...it just wouldn't be Christmas without it.

2 c. crispy corn cereal	6 t. butter, melted
2 c. crispy wheat cereal	3-1/2 T. Worcestershire sauce
2 c. crispy rice cereal	1-1/2 t. seasoned salt
2 c. doughnut-shaped oat cereal	3/4 t. garlic powder
1 c. pretzel sticks	1/2 t. onion powder
1 c. halved pecans	

In a gallon plastic zipping bag, mix together cereals, pretzels and pecans. To melted butter, add Worcestershire sauce and seasonings; stir to mix. Pour in plastic zipping bag, secure bag and shake to coat. Spoon mix on a baking sheet and bake at 250 degrees for one hour; stirring every 15 minutes. Cool and store in an airtight container. Makes 10 cups.

Make gourmet coffee by simply adding a few drops of almond, mint, cinnamon or other flavoring to the coffee once you've scooped it into the coffee maker basket...so easy.

Tree-trimming Treats

Gingery Almond Punch

Carol Ehresman
Ossineke, MI

Add a pretty garnish of lemon or orange zest curls.

6-oz. can frozen lemonade
6-oz. can frozen orange juice
8 c. water
1/2 c. sugar

1/2 t. vanilla extract
1/2 t. almond extract
2-ltr. bottle ginger ale

Combine lemonade, orange juice, water, sugar, vanilla and almond extracts in a punch bowl. Continue to stir until juices have thawed. Add ginger ale to taste and serve with ice. Makes about 30 servings.

Sparkling Punch

Julie Smetzer
Columbus, OH

An ice ring really adds shimmer to a punch bowl. Try making one with whole cranberries, lemon and lime slices.

1 qt. cranberry juice
1 qt. pineapple juice

1-1/2 c. sugar
2 qts. ginger ale, chilled

Combine juices with sugar; stirring well until sugar dissolves. Chill mixture and add ginger ale just before serving. Makes one gallon.

How does Santa leave presents if you don't have a chimney? "You leave a special key on your porch that only Santa can use. No one else can use it but Santa. It's a magic key!"

Elizabeth, age 7

Pineapple Chicken Wings

Robin Kittridge
Elk River, MN

My Great-Grandpa Bruno made these wings every time there was a family get together. Now, I make them for my family...sometimes tripling the recipe just to make sure I get a couple!

1/2 c. sugar	1 t. ground ginger
1/2 c. water	1/2 t. garlic salt
1/2 c. soy sauce	2 t. brown sugar, packed
1/2 c. pineapple juice	2 to 3 lbs. frozen chicken wings,
2 T. oil	thawed

Whisk together sugar, water, soy sauce, pineapple juice, oil, ginger, garlic salt and brown sugar. Place mixture and chicken wings in a plastic zipping bag and marinate for 2 or 3 days in the refrigerator. Place on a greased 15"x12" baking sheet and bake at 350 degrees for one hour. Makes 6 to 8 servings.

Enjoy a welcoming jingle whenever friends come to visit! String an assortment of bells on a length of ribbon, tying a knot before and after each one. Wind the ribbon around an evergreen wreath, then hang on the front door...instant holiday cheer!

Tree-trimming Treats

Stuffed Meatballs

Suze Eggleston
Meridian, ID

What a terrific new way to enjoy meatballs!

2 lbs. ground beef
6-oz. pkg. stuffing mix, cooked

2 10-3/4 oz. cans cream of
  mushroom soup

Form ground beef into 10 to 12 patties, then place one to
2 tablespoons of stuffing into the center of each. Press meat around
the stuffing forming a large meatball. Place meatballs into an
ungreased 13"x9" baking dish. Bake at 350 degrees for 35 to
45 minutes or until meatballs are brown; drain. In a medium
saucepan, heat soup according to can directions; pour over meatballs.
Bake an additional 20 minutes. Makes 10 to 12 meatballs.

A jar filled with peppermints, buttons, rosehips or marbles
makes a delightful votive holder. Scatter several on
your buffet table or line them up along the porch steps
to light the way for guests.

Sour Cream-Ham Dip

Amy Jean Wolfe
Marysville, WA

So good, this has become a "must have" at all family gatherings.

1 c. sour cream
1/2 c. mayonnaise
1/4 t. Worcestershire sauce

1/2 t. garlic salt
1/8 t. pepper
1 c. cooked ham, chopped

Combine all ingredients well and chill for one hour before serving.
Makes 2-1/2 cups.

Cheesy Bites

Angie Floyd
Loveland, OH

I can never keep enough of these on hand...they disappear!

2 lbs. ground beef
8-oz. pkg. pasteurized process
  cheese spread, cubed

1/8 t. fresh oregano, chopped
2 loaves sliced party rye bread

In a large skillet, brown ground beef; drain. Add cheese and oregano;
combine until well blended. Spread mixture onto bread slices and place
onto an ungreased baking sheet. Bake at 350 degrees for 10 minutes.
Makes 30 servings.

For a magical glow, slip some floating candles in a
water-filled red enamelware bowl.

Tree-trimming Treats

Savory Rye Snacks

Linda Hendrix
Moundville, MO

Make this spread the night before and refrigerate. Before your guests arrive, just spread on rye slices and bake.

1 c. green onion, sliced
1 c. mayonnaise
2 c. shredded Colby Jack cheese
4-oz. can sliced mushrooms,
   drained and chopped

2-1/4 oz. can sliced black olives,
   drained and chopped
1 loaf sliced party rye bread

Blend together onion, mayonnaise, cheese, mushrooms and olives. Spread on bread slices and place on an ungreased baking sheet. Bake at 350 degrees for 8 to 10 minutes or until bubbly. Makes 4 dozen.

How do Santa & Mrs. Claus decorate their home?
"Like a cookie house."

Tyler, age 6

41

Salami Cornucopias

SueMary Burford-Smith
Tulsa, OK

For added variety, use slices of prosciutto or roast beef.

12 oz. cream cheese
1 T. mayonnaise
1-1/2 T. Dijon mustard
1 t. seasoned salt
1/4 t. garlic powder

celery salt to taste
3 T. fresh parsley, minced
50 thin slices deli salami
50 gherkin pickles

Combine cream cheese, mayonnaise, mustard, seasoned salt, garlic powder, celery salt and parsley. Spoon cream cheese mixture in the center of each salami slice; place a slice of pickle at one end. Fold salami over forming a cornucopia; secure with a toothpick. Cover and chill for 2 hours. Makes 50 appetizers.

Quick & easy appetizers...cut fresh bagels with a mini star cookie cutter and top with your favorite spread, wrap pear slices with prosciutto or melon wedges with thinly sliced turkey...yum!

Tree-trimming Treats

Artichoke-Parmesan Squares

Mary Webb
Montgomery, AL

*Filled with so many tasty ingredients, this is sure to be a hit
when you serve it to family & friends.*

1-1/2-oz. pkg. vegetable soup
   mix, divided
1/2 c. mayonnaise
1/2 c. sour cream
2 8-oz. pkgs. refrigerated
   crescent roll dough
10-oz. pkg. frozen, chopped
   spinach, thawed and drained
14-oz. can artichoke hearts,
   drained and chopped

8-oz. can water chestnuts,
   drained and chopped
4 oz. feta cheese, crumbled
2 to 3 cloves garlic, pressed
1/2 c. pine nuts, toasted and
   chopped
1/4 c. fresh Parmesan cheese,
   grated

Blend together half the dry soup mix, mayonnaise and sour cream; set
aside. Use remaining soup mix for another recipe. Unroll packages of
crescent dough on a greased 16"x11" baking sheet. Seal perforations
of dough and press dough up sides of sheet to form a crust. Bake at
375 degrees for 10 to 12 minutes or until golden. Add spinach,
artichokes and water chestnuts to mayonnaise mixture; stir in feta
cheese and garlic cloves. Fold in pine nuts and spread mixture over
crust. Sprinkle with Parmesan cheese. Bake an additional 10 to
12 minutes or until heated through. Cut in 2-inch squares. Makes
about 4 dozen.

Christmas Cheese Balls

Karen Wardle
Salt Lake City, UT

Try shaping these into mini bite-size cheese balls, too.

2 8-oz. pkgs. cream cheese
1/4 c. onion, chopped
1/4 c. green pepper, diced
1/2 c. crushed pineapple
1/4 c. maraschino cherries, diced
1 t. garlic salt
1 t. onion salt

1 T. Worcestershire sauce
1 t. seasoned salt
1 c. chopped pecans
2 T. fresh parsley, chopped
Garnish: holly leaves and
    maraschino cherries

Blend cream cheese, onion, green pepper, pineapple, cherries, garlic salt, onion salt, Worcestershire sauce and seasoned salt together. Shape into 3 balls. Roll in pecans and parsley. Top with a holly leaf and cherry.

Kids will love finding treats inside old-fashioned paper crackers. Quick to make...fill a cardboard tube with candy and confetti, wrap in tissue paper and secure the ends with ribbon.

44

Tree-trimming Treats

Parmesan-Bacon Dip

Brenda Sikes
Lindale, TX

Try serving as a dip for shrimp as well as fresh veggies.

2 8-oz. pkgs. cream cheese,
   softened
1/3 c. grated Parmesan cheese
1/3 c. green pepper, diced
1/2 c. green onion, chopped

1/2 c. mayonnaise-type salad
   dressing
10 slices bacon, crisply cooked
   and crumbled

In a medium mixing bowl, blend together all ingredients; chill before
serving. Makes about 3 cups.

Stuffed Mushrooms

Jeannine Reed
Troy, OH

*Substitute any favorite cheese...tomato-basil, Swiss or
herb & garlic all taste great.*

1 lb. ground sausage, uncooked
1 onion, finely chopped
8-oz. pkg. shredded Cheddar
   cheese

24-oz. pkg. mushrooms, stems
   removed

In a large mixing bowl, combine sausage, onion and cheese; stuff
mushroom caps. Place in a greased 13"x9" baking dish and bake at
350 degrees for 20 minutes. Makes 2 to 3 dozen appetizers.

Golden Puffs

Ronni Hall
Chico, CA

Add a little more cayenne pepper if you like a hot flavor!

2 c. shredded Cheddar cheese
1 c. all-purpose flour
1/2 t. paprika
1/4 lb. butter

1/8 t. cayenne
3 to 4 doz. small, stuffed green
olives

Combine first 5 ingredients; mix well and refrigerate until chilled. Shape into walnut-size balls; make an impression in the center of dough and insert an olive. Shape dough around it to fully cover olive. Place puffs on an ungreased baking sheet. Bake at 400 degrees for 10 to 15 minutes or until pastry is golden, but not brown. Makes 16 to 18 servings.

Use T-pins to attach bright woolly mittens to a straw wreath, fill in any empty spaces with greenery sprigs or holly berries...charming!

Tree-trimming Treats

Quick Crab Appetizers

Lynda Purvis
Anchorage, AK

We dropped in to visit friends and before we knew it, we were served these wonderful appetizers...I just had to have the recipe.

6-oz. can crab, well drained
1/2 c. unsalted butter, softened
8-oz. jar sharp pasteurized
    process cheese spread

12 sourdough English muffins,
halved

In a medium mixing bowl, combine crab, butter and cheese together; spread on muffin halves. Lay halves on a ungreased baking sheet and place under broiler, 3 inches from heat source, for 3 to 4 minutes or until golden and bubbling. Cut muffins into quarters and serve hot. Makes 8 dozen appetizers.

Look for unusual containers to hide gifts in...a vintage bread box, lunch pail or watering can!

47

Shrimp & Bacon Bites

Denise Hessier
Paw Paw, MI

Stir in sliced water chestnuts for a delicious crunch!

1 c. cooked shrimp, peeled and
    deveined
1/2 clove garlic, thinly sliced

1/2 c. chili sauce
8 to 10 slices bacon, halved

In a small mixing bowl, combine shrimp and garlic; pour chili sauce over. Cover and refrigerate for several hours, stir occasionally. Wrap each shrimp in a bacon slice; secure with a toothpick. Place on an ungreased baking sheet and broil 3 to 4 inches from heat source for 3 to 5 minutes or until crisp. Makes 16 to 20 bites.

Chubby snowmen add a whimsical touch to your holiday wreath. Just coat round foam balls with white paint, then lightly dust with white glitter while still wet. When dry, paint on eyes and a mouth, add cloves for buttons and a toothpick nose. Glue or wire to a wreath...how fun!

Tree-trimming Treats

Southwest Potato Skins

Pat Habiger
Spearville, KS

The kids love to snack on these while watching movies.

6 potatoes
1 lb. ground beef
1/2 c. onion, chopped
1 t. salt
1 t. pepper
1-1/4 oz. pkg. taco seasoning

2 12-oz. pkgs. shredded
   Cheddar cheese
12-oz. pkg. shredded mozzarella
   cheese, divided
Garnish: chives, bacon bits and
   sour cream

Bake potatoes at 450 degrees for one hour, or until potatoes are tender. Cut in half lengthwise and scoop out center of each potato, leaving 1/4-inch around edges. Save centers of potatoes for another recipe. In a large skillet, brown ground beef with onion, salt and pepper; drain. Add taco seasoning and simmer. Place potato halves in a greased 15"x12" baking dish. Sprinkle with half of Cheddar cheese and 2 tablespoons ground beef, then top with mozzarella and remaining Cheddar cheese. Broil 3 to 4 inches from heat source until cheese is bubbly. Sprinkle on chives, bacon bits and sour cream. Makes 12 potato skins.

It's not a bad little tree. All it needs is a little love.
-Linus Van Pelt
A Charlie Brown Christmas

Party Links

Heather Harrelson
Killeen, TX

Just toss the ingredients in the slow cooker and by the time you finish trimming the tree, they'll be ready to nibble on.

12-oz. jar chili sauce
18-oz. jar grape jam or jelly

20-oz. pkg. sausage links

Place all ingredients in a 4-quart slow cooker. Cook on low for 2 hours or until heated through. Makes 24 appetizers.

People Chow

Janell Rand
Coon Rapids, MN

One of those snacks you just can't quit munching on!

1/2 c. butter
1 c. creamy peanut butter
2 c. milk chocolate chips

17-1/2 oz. pkg. crispy corn and
   rice cereal
1 lb. powdered sugar

Combine butter, peanut butter and chocolate chips in a saucepan. Melt over medium heat, stirring often. Pour over cereal and mix until thoroughly coated. Place cereal in a paper sack, sprinkle in powdered sugar. Fold down the top of the paper sack and shake well. Makes 3 pounds or about 12 servings.

I wish we could put up some of the Christmas spirit in jars and open a jar of it every month.

–Harlan Miller

Tree-trimming Treats

Charleston Cheese Dip

Barbara Bongiorno
Jacksonville, FL

A group of friends created this amazing recipe!

1 c. mayonnaise
2 c. shredded Cheddar cheese
2 8-oz. pkgs. cream cheese,
   softened
4 green onions, sliced

14 round, buttery crackers,
   crushed
1 lb. sliced bacon, crisply cooked
   and crumbled

Mix mayonnaise, cheeses and green onion together. Spread in a
9"x9" baking dish coated with non-stick vegetable spray. Top with
crackers and bake at 350 degrees for 10 to 15 minutes. Add bacon
and allow to sit for 2 to 3 minutes before serving. Makes 30 to
32 servings.

Use a watering can, enamelware pot or painted bucket to
hold a small evergreen or feather tree, they're
just the right size.

51

Maple Hot Chocolate

Peg Baker
La Rue, OH

*Nothing's better after a chilly day of sledding...this will
warm you up head-to-toe.*

1/4 c. sugar	4 c. milk
1 T. baking cocoa	1 t. maple flavoring
1/8 t. salt	1 t. vanilla extract
1/4 c. hot water	12 marshmallows, divided
1 T. butter	

Stir together sugar, cocoa and salt in a saucepan. Add hot water and
butter; bring to a boil. Blend in milk, maple flavoring, vanilla and
8 marshmallows. Heat through, stirring occasionally, until
marshmallows have melted. Serve in mugs and top each with
a marshmallow. Makes 4 servings.

There will be plenty of rosy cheeks after the kids go
caroling...warm them up with a winter tailgate party!
Serve hot cocoa, spiced cider and lots of
homemade cookies, they'll love it.

Tree-trimming Treats

Apple-Cinnamon Punch

Kathy Grashoff
Fort Wayne, IN

*Hosting an open house? Make this punch for
everyone to enjoy...it has a great spicy taste!*

1 c. water
1/2 c. sugar
1/2 c. red cinnamon candies

2 2-ltr. bottles raspberry ginger
  ale, chilled
46-oz. can apple juice, chilled

Combine water, sugar and candies in a small saucepan; bring to a boil.
Reduce heat and simmer, uncovered, for 5 minutes or until candies
melt; stir occasionally. When mixture has cooled, combine with ginger
ale and apple juice; stir well. Makes 25 cups.

Ever had Sugar-on-Snow? Gather a pail of freshly fallen
snow, spoon it into serving bowls and top with warm
maple syrup. A wonderful New England
wintertime treat!

53

Italian Pizza Dip

Valerie Gapen
Wanyesburg, PA

You can use any of your favorite pizza toppings for this dip...ham, pepperoni or mushrooms. Served with warm bread sticks, this will be a hit!

8-oz. cream cheese, softened
2 T. Italian seasoning
3/4 c. mozzarella cheese, divided
2 T. Romano cheese

1 c. pizza sauce
3 T. green pepper, chopped
1 T. green onion, chopped

Blend cream cheese and Italian seasoning together; spread in an 8" round pan. Top with 1/2 cup mozzarella, Romano cheese, pizza sauce, green pepper, green onion and remaining mozzarella. Bake at 375 degrees for 20 minutes, or until hot and bubbly. Makes 10 to 12 servings.

What do the reindeer and elves do after Christmas is over?
"They love to grow flowers inside so it seems warmer to them since it's always winter...Mrs. Claus loves spring flowers."

Nikki, age 5

Tree-trimming Treats

Warm Spinach Dip

Jeannette Zuvich
Hagerstown, MD

You'll be surprised at how many people love this dip, but never imagined they'd like artichokes! Use tortilla chips or buttery crackers for dipping.

13-oz. can artichoke hearts, chopped
10-oz. pkg. frozen chopped spinach, thawed and drained
1 c. mayonnaise

1 c. grated Parmesan cheese
2-1/4 c. grated Monterey Jack cheese, divided
1 T. grated Romano cheese

Stir artichoke hearts, spinach, mayonnaise, Parmesan cheese, 1-3/4 cup Monterey Jack cheese and Romano cheese together until well blended. Spoon in a 2-quart baking dish; top with remaining Monterey Jack cheese. Bake at 350 degrees for 20 to 30 minutes or until cheese is melted. Makes 8 to 10 servings.

Slide a candy cane stick in the center of a foam ball, then cover the ball with peppermint candies. Secure the candy stick in a festive terra cotta pot filled with florists' foam...a sweet topiary!

55

Tiny Sock Ornaments

Melanie Moore
Fremont, IN

Over the years I've saved the tiny socks my children wore as babies...sentimental ornaments for our Christmas tree.

baby booties or socks
1/8-inch ribbon
needle

thread
red and white cross-stitch floss

Cut a length of ribbon one to 2 inches long. Form in a loop and stitch inside the top and back of the bootie or sock. Using cross-stitch floss, add a simple snowflake or heart design on the front of the bootie, or even a name or the year the booties were worn.

Tiny baby booties, mittens, hats and stuffed animals are
sweet decorations for a holiday tree
filled with memories.

Tree-trimming Treats

Gingerbread Wreath

Cassandra Skaggs
Valencia, CA

Set your punch bowl in the middle of this fragrant gingerbread wreath...fun!

1 c. shortening
1 c. brown sugar, packed
3 eggs, beaten
1-1/2 c. molasses
6 c. all-purpose flour
1-1/2 T. ground ginger

2-1/4 t. salt
1-1/2 t. baking soda
1 t. cinnamon
leaf-shaped cookie cutters
water
powdered sugar

Cream together shortening and brown sugar; add eggs and molasses. Sift together dry ingredients and add to egg mixture. Roll out dough and cut leaf shapes using various size and shapes of leaf cookie cutters. You can also use a knife to make veins in the leaves. On an ungreased baking sheet, overlap cookies in a wreath shape, using water to glue the cookies onto one another. Bake at 350 degrees for 15 minutes or until cookies are crisp and golden. Cool overnight on rack and let the wreath set out until hardened, this may take a day or two. If you'd like a snowy look, handle the wreath carefully and stand it at an angle over sheets of newspaper and dust with powdered sugar.

What's your favorite treat to leave Santa and why?
"Cookies, because he told me he likes them most."

Nikki, age 5

57

Magical Ice Ornaments

Kathy Grashoff
Ft. Wayne, IN

*These look so beautiful floating in your punch bowl...your guests
will rave over them!*

round plastic ornaments that
separate
distilled water

cranberries, sliced lemons, limes
and oranges

Rinse ornaments thoroughly; let dry. Pour distilled water into a
large bowl. Place fruit in both sides of ornaments; hold under water
in bowl and allow water to fill inside of ornament as you close it. If
your ornament doesn't have a hole on top to allow for expansion
as the water freezes, leave a space so the ornament won't break.
Place ornaments, hanger end up, in freezer on a dish towel-lined
baking sheet, freeze overnight. To release ornaments, hold under cold
running water and remove from plastic. Place in punch before serving.

Try freezing a favorite fruit juice in ice ornaments
along with some sprigs of fresh rosemary or mint.

Tree-trimming Treats

Cheerful Cookie Jar

Gail Byker
Gurnee, IL

One year, my sister gave me a large glass jar to fill with Christmas cookies I'd made for my daughters. After the holidays, I didn't want to pack it away, so I came up with an idea to enjoy it year 'round!

large clear glass cookie jar   sponge
acrylic paints   paint brushes
dish soap   ribbon

Wash jar inside and out; dry completely. In a bowl, mix together equal parts of acrylic paint and dish soap. Dip sponge in paint and paint a scene on your jar...snowmen, Christmas trees or a wreath would be terrific. Add the smaller details to your jar with a paint brush. Set aside until paint is dry, then tie a ribbon around the top of the jar. When you want to change the scene on your cookie jar, just wash in hot, soapy water and start again!

What a clever gift...give this cookie jar already painted and filled with tubes of paint, several brushes, a sponge and the above instructions!

Windowbox Snow Family

*Zoe Bennett
Columbia, SC*

*Windowboxes aren't just for summertime displays. Greet your
family & friends with a whimsical family of snowmen!*

snowman-shaped wooden
   cutouts
white, black and orange acrylic
   paint
matte sealer
wide and fine point paint
   brushes

fabric scraps
hot glue
buttons
twigs
florist's foam
evergreen sprigs
holly branches

Paint snowman cutouts with white paint using a wide paint brush; let
dry. Apply a second coat if needed. Add orange nose, black eyes and
mouth with a fine point paint brush; let dry. Spray with 2 or 3 coats of
matte sealer to protect paint; let dry well between each coat. Tie fabric
scraps on for scarves and use hot glue to add buttons and twigs for
arms. Secure twigs to backs of snowmen with hot glue; let set. Cut
florist's foam to fit windowbox and tuck snowmen securely in foam.
Cover top of foam with evergreen sprigs and holly branches.

*If you don't have a windowbox, tuck these jolly
snowmen on a wreath, in a basket or berry bucket.*

Tree-trimming Treats

"Dear Santa" Pillows

Connie Brooks
Council Bluffs, IA

Sure to give your friends & family the giggles!

20"x12" tea-dyed muslin
embroidery hoop
embroidery floss or fabric pen
needle
straight pins

20"x12" homespun
polyester fiberfill
6"x1" homespun
small safety pin

Press muslin and position in embroidery hoop. Use embroidery floss to stitch or fabric pen to write "Dear Santa...I can explain" on the muslin. Pin muslin and homespun, right sides together. Machine stitch around 3 sides, trim and turn right side out; press. Stuff pillow with polyester fiberfill and machine or handstitch last side together. Tear a length of homespun 6 inches long and tie in a bow. Pin or stitch to a corner of the pillow.

When Santa & Mrs. Claus take a vacation, where do they go?
"Disney World to buy presents
for next Christmas."

Austin, age 7

Red Mitten Valance

Liz Marcellin
Newark, CA

*A sweet decoration that would make a darling tree
or mantel garland, too.*

clothesline
2 cup hooks
children's mittens

clothes pins
holly sprigs

Measure the length of your window, adding 4 inches. To secure clothesline, insert cup hooks at the upper corners of the window. Place the clothesline in the center of the window, letting it droop just a little in the middle. Wrap the extra 2 inches on each end around the cup hooks then tie in a knot. Attach several mittens to clothesline with clothespins then tuck holly sprigs inside.

What kind of snacks do reindeer like?
"Apples because they like
the fruity taste."

Ryan, age 6

62

Tree-trimming Treats

Holiday Garden Swag

Patricia Husek
St. Joseph, MI

This clever winter welcome can be made especially for gardeners, bakers or artists!

trowel, spade and garden fork
heavy-duty wire
evergreen boughs

2-inch wide ribbon
green wax-coated string or
pipe cleaners

Tie all garden tools together securely with wire, forming a loop in the back for hanging. Lay tools on several evergreen boughs, keeping them in place with additional wire. Add fullness to the front of the swag by tucking some smaller greenery sprigs around the tools. Form a ribbon bow and secure around the greenery stems with green wax-coated string or pipe cleaners.

Christmas is not in tinsel and lights...it's lighting a fire inside the heart.

-Wilfred A. Peterson

Jolly Get-togethers

Gather friends & family together for a tree-trimming party...it's a fun way to start the holiday season. Serve food buffet-style with lots of finger foods and appetizers. Set out plates of cookies and sweets, festive punch, eggnog and cocoa. Don't forget to play all the best Christmas songs, too. Everyone will be laughing, having a great time, and before you know it, the tree will be trimmed!

Host a weekend brunch...a great break from all the evening parties we go to this time of year. Offer a selection of fresh fruit, bagels, tasty breakfast casseroles, muffins, coffee, juice and chamomile tea.

A caroling party is terrific for both kids and adults! Make copies of sheet music and get in a little practice before you go...piling everyone in a hay wagon adds to the fun and neighbors will love it! Be sure to take along lots of blankets and hot cocoa for keeping warm.

How about going ice skating? Even if you haven't done it since you were little, it's a great way to get families together. There will be lots of laugher...guaranteed!

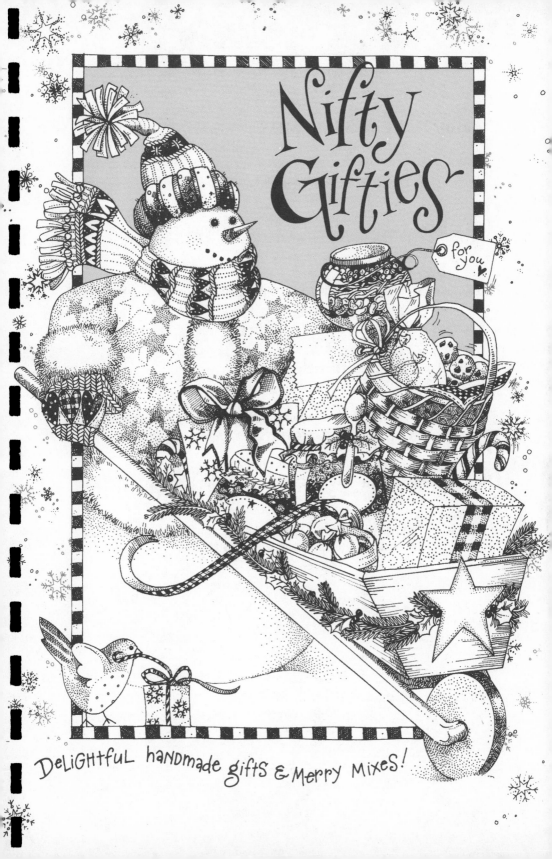

Nifty Gifties

for you ♥

DeLightful handmade gifts & Merry Mixes!

Creamy Hot Chocolate Mix

Tracy Schaffner
Altoona, IA

For snowy days, this is our family's tradition.

1 lb. chocolate drink mix
1-1/4 c. powdered non-dairy
    creamer

25.6-oz. pkg. powdered milk
2 c. powdered sugar

In a large mixing bowl, combine all ingredients and store in an airtight container. Give with these instructions: To serve add desired amount of mix to 8 ounces hot water or milk. Makes about 29 cups mix.

Peppermint Marshmallows

Lisa Schorr
Lancaster, OH

You can also make cinnamon marshmallows. Just eliminate the peppermint extract and add 2 teaspoons of cinnamon.

1 t. peppermint extract
3/4 c. powdered sugar

10-1/2 oz. pkg. mini
    marshmallows

In a plastic zipping bag, shake together peppermint extract and powdered sugar. Add marshmallows and toss to coat.

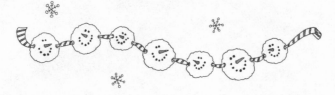

Great for a kid's tree...a snowman garland! Cut out circles with decorative-edge scissors and paint on a smiling face. Use a hole punch to make a hole on each side of the circle, then string on ribbon.

Nifty Gifties

Cheery Cappuccino Mix

Jackie Mattus
Oregon, IL

Fill a plastic zipping bag with cappuccino mix, nestle in a deep coffee mug and tie on some coffee stir sticks...a coffee lover's dream!

2/3 c. plus 1 t. instant coffee granules
1-1/4 c. powdered non-dairy creamer
1 c. chocolate drink mix
1/2 c. sugar

1/2 t. cinnamon
1/4 t. nutmeg
2-1/2 plus 1/8 c. powdered milk
1 t. salt
1-3/4 c. powdered sugar

In a blender, grind coffee granules to a fine powder. Combine all ingredients in a large mixing bowl; blend well. Store in airtight container. Attach the following directions to mix: Use 3 heaping teaspoons per cup or mug of hot water; adjust as needed. Makes about 7 cups of mix.

Instead of using gingerbread to make a house, try stacking sugar cubes. "Glue" them together with royal icing for a sparkling winter wonderland!

Onion Soup Mix

Iva Anderson
Tuscon, AZ

There are endless recipes for this popular mix!

3/4 c. dried, minced onion
1/3 c. beef flavor bouillon
   granules

4 t. onion powder
1/4 t. celery seed, crushed
1/2 t. sugar

Combine all ingredients and store in an airtight container, makes
20 tablespoons of mix. Add these recipe cards when giving as a gift:
To Make Roasted Potatoes: Toss 5 tablespoons soup mix with 6 peeled
and cubed potatoes and 1/3 cup olive oil. Spoon on a 15"x10" baking
sheet and bake at 450 degrees for 35 to 40 minutes or until potatoes
are tender. To Make Onion Soup: Combine 4 cups water with
5 tablespoons soup mix; bring to a boil. Simmer, uncovered, for
10 minutes. To Make Onion Dip: blend 5 tablespoons mix with 2 cups
sour cream. Stir well and refrigerate at least 2 hours. Stir again before
serving with fresh vegetables or potato chips.

Treat yourself to snowflakes that won't melt! Draw or
trace a snowflake design on paper and lay a square
of parchment paper on top. Trace the design by piping
on royal icing, sprinkle with edible white glitter and let
dry. Peel off the parchment paper for a
shimmering dessert dish garnish!

Nifty Gifties

Mexican Bean Soup Mix

Michelle Campen
Peoria, IL

Cut a square of bright yellow fabric to fit over your jar lid and stencil on red and green chili peppers for a festive southwestern feel!

3/4 c. dried pinto beans
3/4 c. dried red kidney beans
2 T. dried onion flakes
2 T. dried parsley
1 T. chili powder
2 t. cumin

1 t. dried oregano
6 cubes chicken bouillon
1/2 c. white rice, uncooked
1 c. wagon wheel pasta,
    uncooked

Place beans in a one-quart, wide-mouth jar. Combine onion flakes, parsley, chili powder, cumin, oregano and chicken bouillon in a small plastic sandwich bag; seal. Place rice and pasta in separate sandwich bags; seal securely. Tuck all bags in quart jar for gift giving and attach the following directions: Rinse and sort beans; place in a large stockpot with 4 cups water. Bring to a boil, cover and remove from heat. Let sit for one hour. Drain beans and return to pot. Add 8 cups water and contents of flavor packet. Bring to a boil; reduce heat, cover and simmer for one hour or until beans are tender. Stir in rice and bring to a simmer. Cover and simmer for 15 minutes. Uncover, stir in pasta and 1/2 cup water. Simmer for 10 minutes or until pasta is tender. Makes 8 to 10 servings.

Paint a round box red and white so it looks like peppermint candy. When dry, fill with a gift mix, wrap the box in cellophane and tie a ribbon on each side...looks like a giant peppermint!

White Chocolate Cookie Mix

Sharon Pruess
South Ogden, UT

Use cinnamon or peanut butter chips for a new twist.

2-1/2 c. all-purpose flour
1 t. baking soda
1/4 t. salt
1/2 c. sugar

1/2 c. chopped pecans
1 c. white chocolate chips
1 c. brown sugar, packed

In a medium mixing bowl, combine flour, baking soda and salt together. Layer sugar, pecans, chocolate chips, brown sugar and flour mixture into a one-quart wide-mouth canning jar. Press each layer firmly in place before adding the next ingredient. Attach the following directions to mix: Empty jar of cookie mix into a large mixing bowl; stir to blend. Add 1-1/2 sticks of softened butter, one egg; beaten, and one teaspoon vanilla extract. Mix until completely blended. Shape into walnut-size balls and place 2 inches apart on baking sheet. Bake at 350 degrees for 10 minutes. Makes 2-1/2 dozen cookies.

A friend who bakes would love to find a cookbook slipped in the pocket of a potholder. Don't forget to tuck in recipe cards sharing some family favorites, too.

Nifty Gifties

Double Chip-Walnut Brownie Mix

Shelly Pitsch
Billings, MT

Turn these into chocolatey mint brownies by just adding mint chocolate chips instead of vanilla chips.

1/3 c. baking cocoa	2/3 c. brown sugar, packed
2/3 c. sugar	1-1/3 c. all-purpose flour
1/2 c. chocolate chips	1 t. salt
1/2 c. vanilla chips	1/2 c. chopped walnuts

Layer cocoa in a one-quart, wide-mouth canning jar. Use a paper towel to remove any cocoa from sides of jar. Layer in remaining ingredients; sugar, chocolate chips, vanilla chips, brown sugar, flour, salt and walnuts. Be sure to press down each layer as tightly as possible before adding the next. Attach the following directions to the jar: Combine jar ingredients with one teaspoon vanilla extract, 2/3 cup oil and 3 eggs. Pour into a greased 9"x9" baking pan. Bake at 350 degrees for 25 to 30 minutes. Makes 9 servings.

What are your favorite things to do during Christmas? "We like to help Mom make cookies and decorate. Then we eat all the cookies!"

Kyle & Sean, ages 6 and 3

Homemade Doggie Biscuits

*Sammy Polizzi-Morrison
Centennial, CO*

*Stir in a little beef bouillon with the water or toss in
some bacon bits for extra flavor.*

3/4 c. hot water
1/3 c. margarine
1/2 c. powdered milk
1/2 t. salt

2 t. sugar
1 egg, beaten
3 c. whole-wheat flour

In a large mixing bowl, pour hot water over margarine. Stir in
powdered milk, salt, sugar and egg. Add flour, 1/2 cup at a time,
mixing well after each addition. Knead for 4 to 5 minutes, adding
more flour if necessary to make a stiff dough. Roll to 1/2-inch
thickness and cut out with a bone shaped cookie cutter; hearts or cat
shapes would be fun, too. Place on a greased baking sheet. Bake at
325 degrees for 45 minutes. Allow to cool completely. Makes about
3 dozen, depending on the size of cookie cutter.

Kitties deserve treats, too. Fish-shaped cookie cutters
turn this recipe into the "purrfect" tidbit!

Nifty Gifties

Treat Jar
Vickie

Filled with homemade biscuits...any pet lover will be delighted!

one-gallon pantry jar
paint brush
acrylic paint
medium tip paint brush

clear acrylic spray sealer
cat or dog collar the same
diameter as jar lid

Wash and thoroughly dry jar and lid; set aside jar. Paint lid with acrylic paint, let dry and apply a second coat. Using a paint brush with a medium tip, add your pet's name to the top of the jar, or even scatter on some phrases..."Pampered Pet", "Here, Kitty, Kitty" or "Treats for a good boy." When the paint has completely dried, protect it with a coat with sealer. Allow sealer to dry, then secure the collar around the neck of the jar or on the lid rim.

How does Santa leave presents if you don't have a chimney?
"He uses his magic powers in his hands to open the door. If he runs out of electricity and his magic powers don't work, then he can use his magic key...it takes batteries."

Austin, age 4

Cinnamon Stick Button Tree

Louise Schulze
Troy, OH

Slip in a basket with a gift mix...a little extra surprise.

1 small foam ball
1-1/2 to 2-inch tall terra cotta
   pot
6-inch cinnamon stick
glue gun and glue
moss

17 inches of 1/2-inch artificial
   wide pine roping
1" dia. wooden star
yellow ochre acrylic paint
assorted buttons

Glue a small foam ball into terra cotta pot. Make a hole in the center of the foam ball with the end of cinnamon stick. Hot glue the end of the cinnamon stick into the hole. Glue enough moss around the base of the cinnamon stick to cover foam. Cut pine roping in the following lengths: 3-1/2 inches, 4 inches, 4-1/2 inches and 5 inches. Wrap the center of the 3-1/2 inch piece of pine around the top of the cinnamon stick, securing with hot glue. The length of the branches should be equal on each side. Attach the other branches the same way, about 3/4 inch apart ending with the 5-inch piece at the bottom. Cut a piece of pine roping about one inch long and hot glue vertically to the top of the cinnamon stick. Paint wooden star with yellow ochre acrylic paint; let dry, then glue to the pine branch at the top of the tree. Attach buttons to the ends of the other branches with pearl cotton, crochet thread or hot glue.

Nifty Gifties

Fireplace Pine Cones

Donna Whiteside
Denver, IN

Warm up by a colorful fire and enjoy a tin of your favorite snack mix...a great way to end a day of holiday shopping.

1 bushel pine cones, divided
2 mesh bags
2 plastic buckets
1/2 lb. boric acid

2 gal. water, divided
2 bricks
1 lb. copper sulfate

Divide pine cones in half and place in 2 mesh bags. For pine cones with a green color, dissolve boric acid in one gallon water. You can get boric acid at your local pharmacy. Soak one bag of pine cones, using a rock to hold the bag down, for 3 to 4 days; then let air dry completely. To create a blue-green color, dissolve copper sulfate in the second gallon of water. Copper sulfate can be found at a garden center or hardware store. Soak the second bag of pine cones in this solution, again, holding down with a brick, for 3 to 4 days; let dry. For colorful flames, toss pine cones in a log fire.

It is Christmas in the heart
that puts Christmas in the air.

-W.T. Ellis

Mollohan's Mix

Pat Mollohan
Parkersburg, WV

Looking or a gift for the kids' teachers? A jar of snack mix tucked inside a red tin will be a welcome gift.

1/2 c. dried apples
1/2 c. walnut pieces
1/2 c. dried pears

1/2 c. colorful, candy-coated
   chocolate mini baking bits
1/2 c. dried bananas

In a one-pint, wide-mouth canning jar, layer apples, walnuts, pears, mini baking bits and bananas in order listed. Makes 4 to 6 servings.

Sugared Nuts

Michelle Campen
Peoria, IL

Crunchy nuts with a sweet, cinnamon coating!

1 egg white
1 c. sugar
1-1/4 t. cinnamon
1/2 t. allspice
1/4 t. nutmeg

1/4 t. ground ginger
1/8 t. coriander
1 lb. whole almonds

In a large mixing bowl, beat egg white and sugar together; add cinnamon, allspice, nutmeg, ginger and coriander. Toss nuts in egg white mixture and spread on an ungreased baking sheet. Bake at 200 degrees for one hour, stirring nuts every 15 minutes to prevent sticking. Once cool, place spiced nuts in decorative jars or tins. Makes one pound.

Christmas isn't a season...it's a feeling.

-Edna Ferber

Nifty Gifties

Cake in a Cup Mix

Cari Baker
Wayland, NY

Great for college students…a sweet treat anytime. Try different combinations to get your favorite flavors.

18-1/2 oz. box chocolate cake mix
3-1/2 oz. pkg. instant chocolate pudding mix

3 c. powdered sugar, divided
4-1/2 T. hot cocoa mix, divided
2-1/4 t. vanilla powder, divided

Place dry cake mix and pudding mix in a large mixing bowl; mix together. Divide and place 1/2 cup mix in 8 plastic sandwich bags; secure. Tuck one bag in a large mug that will hold at least 1-1/2 cups of water. Because the cake is microwaved, be sure the cup doesn't have any metal decoration on it. Place 1/3 cup powdered sugar, 1-1/2 teaspoons hot cocoa mix and 1/4 teaspoon vanilla powder into plastic sandwich bags; secure with a twist tie and attach to cake bag labeling as glaze mix. Place one bag of cake and glaze mix each mug and attach the following directions to mix: Generously spray inside of coffee mug with non-stick vegetable spray. Empty contents of cake mix bag into each mug and add one egg white, one tablespoon oil and one tablespoon water. Mix until well blended. Microwave on high for 2 minutes. While cake is baking, place glaze mix into a small mixing bowl and add 1-1/2 teaspoons water; mix well. When cake is done, pour glaze over cake in the cup and enjoy while warm. Makes 8 to 9 cake mixes.

Amaretto Coffee Creamer

Patsy Roberts
Center, TX

Share a jar of coffee creamer in a charming old-fashioned milk bottle.

3/4 c. powdered non-dairy
   creamer
1 t. almond extract

1 t. cinnamon
3/4 c. powdered sugar

In a large mixing bowl, combine all ingredients; mix well to blend.
Store in an airtight container. Attach the following directions to mix:
In a mug or cup, combine 2 tablespoons of creamer with 6 ounces of
brewed coffee. Makes 12 servings.

While shopping at the mall, pile everyone in a photo
booth...have fun! Glue photos to squares of cardstock
to make gift tags or turn color copies
into wrapping paper.

Nifty Gifties

Coffee Stir Sticks

Gail Prather
Bethel, MN

Each year I make gift baskets for my friends & family. I always include these stir sticks along with some flavorful coffee beans.

1 c. sugar
1/3 c. brewed coffee
1 T. corn syrup
1/4 t. baking cocoa
1/4 t. cinnamon

1/2 t. vanilla extract
12 wooden craft sticks
cellophane
ribbon

In a large saucepan, combine sugar, coffee, corn syrup, cocoa and cinnamon. Cook over medium heat until the sugar dissolves, stirring constantly. Continue to cook over medium heat, without stirring, until a candy thermometer reaches 290 degrees for about 7 minutes. Remove from heat and add vanilla; stir well. Pour into a greased 2-cup glass measuring cup. Working quickly, pour tablespoonfuls into circles on a greased baking sheet and lay a stick in each circle. Allow to cool at room temperature until hardened. When cooled, wrap with cellophane and tie with ribbon. Store in an airtight container. Makes one dozen stir sticks.

What are your favorite things to do during Christmas?
"Wait for gifts and to make a Christmas list."

Ryan, age 6

Tumble Santas

Mel Wolk
St. Peters, MO

Jolly fun...enjoy these on a mantel, windowsill or shelf.

5-1/2 inch wooden star cut from
  one-inch thick pine board
red acrylic paint
skin tone acrylic paint
white acrylic paint

black acrylic paint
paintbrushes
toothpick
clear polyurethane spray sealer
fine sandpaper

Paint entire star in red; let dry. Add Santa face, hat, hands and boots. Make eyes and buttons with handle of paintbrush dipped in black paint. When eyes are dry, dot white highlights in the same spot on each eye with a toothpick. When Santa is completely dry, spray with the polyurethane; allow to dry overnight. Sand edges of the star with sandpaper to give it a worn look.

How does Santa leave presents if you don't have a chimney?
"He comes through the cracks in the door and wiggles his nose, then all the presents magically get bigger."

Nikki, age 5

Nifty Gifties

Handprint Wallhanging

Heidi Newlin
Cherokee, OK

After a day of wintry fun, warm the kids up with some creamy cocoa,
then make this wallhanging Grandma will treasure!

1 yd. unbleached muslin
wax paper
salad plate

sponge brush
green acrylic paint
red acrylic paint

Wash muslin in cold water; dry and iron. Lay on wax paper and place a salad plate in the center. Have kids paint their hands with a sponge brush dipped in acrylic paint. Each child places their handprint on the muslin around the outside of the salad plate, forming a wreath. Red berries may be added with fingertips dipped in paint on his or her own handprints. Two red handprints with thumbs down and together, may be added for a bow or a fabric bow may be used. A holiday greeting can be sponge-painted across the top or have the kids write it in with paint pens, as well as their names and the date.

Add a sparkly touch to garlands...tie on shimmering tin icicles and sweet mitten-shaped cookie cutters.

Gingerbread Men Ornaments

Susan Merritt
Chincoteague Island, VA

Although they're non-edible, they look and smell wonderful tucked in gift baskets or hanging on your Christmas tree.

1 c. shortening
1 c. brown sugar, packed
2 c. molasses
1 c. white glue

1 T. baking soda
1 T. ground ginger
6 to 8 c. all-purpose flour
1-3/4 c. water

Cream shortening with brown sugar; add molasses and glue; set aside. Combine baking soda and ginger with 6 cups flour. Add flour mixture and water alternately to creamed mixture. Add enough remaining flour to make a stiff dough; knead well. Roll to 1/4-inch thickness and cut out with a gingerbread man cookie cutter; place on an ungreased baking sheet. Bake at 300 degrees for one hour or until golden. Repeat with any remaining dough. To thoroughly dry gingerbread men, place them in the oven on oven racks and bake at 100 degrees an additional 3 hours. Let cool completely and frost with royal icing. Makes approximately 2 dozen.

Royal Icing:

2 egg whites
3 c. powdered sugar

1 T. lemon juice
1/4 t. salt

Combine egg whites, powdered sugar, lemon juice and salt; beat at high speed for 2 to 3 minutes or until mixture holds soft peaks. Makes 2 cups frosting.

Christmas! The very word brings joy to our hearts!

—Joan Winmill Brown

Nifty Gifties

Candy Cane Terra Cotta Pot

Tina Ledbetter
Murrieta, CA

Fill with candy canes for a very festive hostess gift.

4-inch terra cotta pot
spray primer

red and white acrylic paint
clear acrylic spray sealer

Paint terra cotta pot with alternating red and white stripes. Paint the saucer red; let both dry thoroughly. Cover with 2 or 3 coats of sealer.

Muffin Tin Crayons

Flo Burtnett
Gage, OK

Crayons that are just the right size for little fingers.

small, broken crayons

Peel the paper from broken crayons and drop similar colors together into miniature non-stick muffin tins. Bake at 350 degrees for 4 to 5 minutes, or until the crayon bits have melted. Remove the pan from the oven and let cool for 5 minutes. Place the pan in the freezer for 10 minutes. Crayons will shrink from sides of pan and easily remove when pan is turned over.

Christmas Jam

Cora Baker
La Rue, OH

Spoon down the center of pancakes, roll up and sprinkle with powdered sugar. Great on French toast or biscuits, too.

3 c. cranberries
1 orange, peeled and seeded
10-oz. pkg. frozen, sliced
    strawberries, slightly thawed
1/4 t. ground cloves

1/4 t. cinnamon
4 c. sugar
1/2 c. water
1 pouch liquid fruit pectin

Combine cranberries and orange quarters in a food processor; pulse until coarsely chopped. Add strawberries, cloves and cinnamon; process until mixture is finely chopped. Stir together fruit mixture, sugar and water in a large saucepan until well blended. Stirring constantly over low heat, cook for 2 minutes. Increase heat to high and bring mixture to a rolling boil; stir in liquid pectin. Stirring constantly bring to a rolling boil again and boil for one minute. Remove from heat; skim off foam. Immediately, pour into 6 hot sterilized half-pint jars. Adjust caps and process for 10 minutes in a boiling water bath. Makes 6 half-pints.

What are your favorite things to do during Christmas?
"I love to go to the zoo to see all the pretty
lights and ice skaters and
drink hot chocolate."

Elizabeth, age 7

Nifty Gifties

Old-Fashioned Apple Butter

Linda Smeiles
Kent, OH

Roll out leftover pie crust, cut in shapes, bake and spread with a little apple butter as a treat for the cook and any little helpers!

1 gal. applesauce	2 t. cinnamon
4-1/2 c. sugar	1 t. ground cloves

Combine all ingredients in a large mixing bowl. Pour in a 6-quart slow cooker, uncovered, on low for 8 to 12 hours; stirring occasionally. After 8 to 12 hours, check the thickness. If apple butter is too thin, continue cooking until it reaches desired thickness. Fill sterilized pint jars, clean rim and place lid and ring on; securing tightly. Process in a boiling water bath for 20 minutes. Remove jars from water, lids should pull down as jars cool. Makes 7 to 9 pints.

Cover the table with giftwrap...what a clever tablecloth and oh, so festive!

Apple Pie in a Jar

Beth Landis
Mentone, IN

*Spoon over vanilla ice cream and sprinkle with cinnamon
for a simple holiday dessert or pour in a pie crust
and bake for a yummy homemade apple pie.*

5 to 6 lbs. apples, sliced	1/4 t. nutmeg
4-1/2 c. sugar	1 t. salt
1 c. cornstarch	10 c. water
2 t. cinnamon	3 T. lemon juice

Pack apples tightly in wide-mouth, one-quart jars. In a large saucepan, cook sugar, cornstarch, cinnamon, nutmeg, salt and water over medium-high heat until thick and bubbly; add lemon juice. Cover apples with syrup, wipe jars well, add lids and tighten down rings. Process for 20 minutes in water bath. Makes 7 quarts.

Thread crab apples on wire, then shape into a heart. Add
a loop of homespun for hanging....so pretty on a
cupboard or pie safe door.

Nifty Gifties

Chocolate Jar Cake

Michelle Campen
Peoria, IL

*Keep several jars in a basket by the door as gifts for friends
who drop by for a holiday visit.*

1 stick plus 3 T. unsalted butter
3 c. sugar, divided
4 eggs
1 T. vanilla extract
2 c. applesauce

3 c. all-purpose flour
3/4 c. baking cocoa
1 t. baking soda
1/2 t. baking powder
1/8 t. salt

In a large mixing bowl, beat together butter and 1-1/2 cups sugar until fluffy. Add eggs and remaining sugar. Add vanilla and applesauce. Sift together dry ingredients in a large mixing bowl; add to cream mixture. Sterilize and dry 8 one-pint, wide-mouth jars. Grease the inside and spoon one cup batter in each; wipe rims clean. Place filled jars on a 13"x9" baking dish. Bake at 325 degrees for 45 minutes to one hour or until center tests done. Sterilize lids in boiling water, place on jars and tighten down rings. Makes 8 pint-size cakes.

Lightly write a holiday greeting on a paper lampshade with a pencil, then use a sharp T-pin to carefully punch through lettering on the shade. When the light is turned on, your message will glow.

Photo Frame Tray

Darlene Strohmeyer
Rice Lake, WI

Share special memories...photos, postcards and notes will make this tray a family keepsake.

spray paint
wooden serving tray
glass
photos
postcards

letters or notes
maps
cardstock
pen
decorative-edge scissors

Spray paint serving tray; set aside until thoroughly dry. Add a second coat if needed. Measure the inside dimensions of the tray and have glass cut to fit. Arrange photos, postcards, letters and maps, or color copies of each, on the tray until you find an arrangement you like. Use the cardstock to jot down favorite quotes or to note the date and occasion of the photos; trim with scissors. Place glass over the photos, maps and postcards to hold them in place and protect them.

Make snowman tie-ons. Paint bells white; let dry and add a cheery face to each. When the paint's dry, slip through several strands of raffia and tie to packages.

Nifty Gifties

Starry Night Oil Lamp

Marsha Kiss
Marysville, OH

So simple, anyone can make this whimsical lamp.

gloss acrylic enamel paint for
    glass
paint brushes
cobalt blue glass water bottle

ceramic top with wick
22-oz. bottle 99.9 percent pure
    paraffin lamp oil

Paint whimsical snowmen, pine trees and snowflakes on the outside
of the bottle; let dry. Make sure your ceramic top with wick fits the
bottle top without slipping inside. Wrap painted bottle, wick and bottle
of lamp oil in tissue and tuck in a gift bag or box with these
instructions: Carefully fill bottle with lamp oil, slip in wick and light.
For best burning, keep oil level at 2/3 or above.

How does Santa leave presents if you don't have a chimney?
"He knocks on the door to wake up
Mom & Dad."

Kelli, age 6

Sweet Treat Jar

Christi Miller
New Paris, PA

Fill with gumdrops and peppermints for friend with a sweet tooth or buttons and bobbins for someone who loves to sew.

one-pint canning jar
15-inch sq. bleached muslin
hot glue
polyester fiberfill
brightly-colored crew sock
jute

black and orange acrylic paint
peppermint candies
homespun or flannel
greenery and berries
assorted buttons

Cut two, 6-inch circles from muslin. Sew circles together with a 1/4-inch seam and leave a 3-inch opening. Clip curves and turn right side out; stuff firmly with fiberfill. Hot glue on top of jar lid. Using the crew sock for the hat; fold up the cuff and hot glue to head. Cut off 4 inches off sock at toe end. Stuff sock lightly next to head. Tie off top 3 inches with jute; cut into 1/2-inch strips. Paint a snowman face with acrylic paint; let dry. Fill jar with goodies, then tighten on lid. Tear a strip of homespun or flannel for a scarf; tie around the neck. Trim his hat or scarf with greenery, berries or buttons.

What are *your* favorite things to do during Christmas?
"Have a snowball fight because I get to throw snow at people."

Conner, age 5

Nifty Gifties

Holly Jolly Potholders

Wendy Jacobs
Idaho Falls, ID

Made with sweet, little handprints, Grandma might keep these potholders for decoration only...they're so cute!

potholders
pencil

red, white and black fabric paint
fine point paint brushes

Place your child's hand in the center of a potholder with fingers together and thumb extended. Using a pencil, lightly trace outside their hand, this will be Santa's beard and hat. Using black fabric paint, paint around the edges to make an outline. Follow the illustration below to create his face and fur trim. Fill in hat with red paint, blend red and white together for pink cheeks and add black dots for eyes. When paint is completely dry, paint a whimsical red and white candy cane strip around the potholder edges, a favorite Christmas verse or your child's name and this year's date.

Give a pail of fun! Fill an enamelware pail with packets of hot cocoa mix, homebaked cookies, popcorn for popping and a classic holiday movie.
Great for snowy days!

Spiced Tea Mix

*Sharon Harris
Herndon, PA*

*Give a friend a charming breakfast basket...nestle in this mix,
some warm biscuits and a jar of homemade preserves.*

1-1/4 c. orange drink mix
3/4 c. sweetened ice tea mix
   with lemon

1 t. cinnamon
1/2 t. allspice
1/4 t. ground cloves

Combine orange drink mix, ice tea mix, cinnamon, allspice and cloves; store in an airtight container. Attach the following directions to mix: For one serving, combine 2 tablespoons of hot tea mix with one cup boiling water in a cup or mug. Makes 16 servings.

Use lots of imagination when giving holiday gift mixes...flavored coffees and teas can be given in a one-of-a-kind teacup, cocoa mix in a nostalgic milk bottle, bread mixes in an ovenproof bread crock and soup mixes in a speckled stockpot.

Nifty Gifties

Apple-Raisin Rice Mix

Jo Ann

*Your friends will love this rice mix filled with dried fruit,
toasted almonds and just a touch of curry.*

3 c. long-grain white rice,
   uncooked
3 T. dried minced onion
1-1/2 T. curry
4 T. chicken bouillon

2 t. salt
1 c. dried apples, chopped
1/3 c. raisins
1/3 c. slivered almonds, toasted

Blend together rice, onion, curry, bouillon, salt, apples, raisins and
almonds. Give in an airtight tin or jar with these instructions: Pour
2 cups water in a 2-quart saucepan and bring to a boil. Add one cup
rice mix slowly, so as to not stop water from boiling, then blend in
2 tablespoons butter. Reduce heat to medium-low and cook, covered,
for 30 minutes or until water is absorbed. Makes about 3-1/2 cups.

What's your favorite treat to leave Santa and why?
"I like to leave gingerbread men cookies
with lots of sprinkles. Santa loves to eat
cookies and I love lots of sprinkles. I also
love eggs & toast...maybe we should
leave him eggs & toast, too."

Austin, age 4

Festive Gift Ideas

Chocolate Lover's Basket...
> A collection of gourmet cocoa, chocolate-dipped peppermint sticks and pretzels, chewy brownies, chocolate-peanut butter fudge, double chocolate cookies and cocoa-dusted truffles.

College Student Survival Kit...
> Fill a waste paper basket with school supplies...scissors, pencils, pens, tape, glue, sticky notes, push pins, paper clips, envelopes, stapler, day planner and a calling card.

Tea-Time Basket...
> A white wicker basket will look pretty filled with a colorful teacup and saucer, a variety of herbal teas, honey and honey dipper, homemade jams, shortbread and a silver teaspoon.

Snow Ice Cream Basket...
> Tuck an ice cream scoop, flavored syrups, sprinkles, jars of marshmallow creme, maraschino cherries and nuts in a Santa hat. Don't forget to add the recipe for snow ice cream!

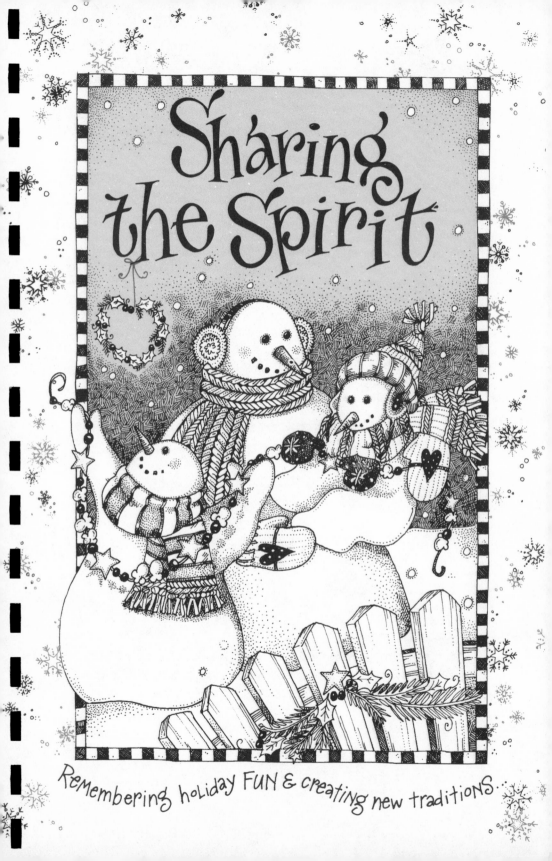

Sharing the Spirit

Remembering holiday FUN & creating new traditions

Stephanie McAtee
Kansas City, MO

Whoever woke up first on Christmas morning, my brother or I, crawled down the hall to the other's room to wake him or her up. We would always go down the hallway single file so we wouldn't be seen or heard by our parents. Sometimes, we'd get caught and sent back to bed, only to wait long enough for them to go to sleep so we could try it again! Once we made it to the living room where the Christmas tree was, we would plug in the lights and look at all of the new gifts placed under the tree just since we had gone to bed...some wrapped and some not. Then, we would dump our stockings to see what all Santa had left inside! We'd lay in front of the tree and talk about what we thought was in all of the packages; comparing the shapes and sizes to what we had asked for. When it was time to wake our parents up, we repeated what we had done hours earlier...dumped our stockings again, and acted if it was the first time we had seen it all!

On Christmas morning...at last we would be called downstairs to a day filled with magic and wonder, a day you hoped would never end.

-John Hadamuscin

Sharing the Spirit

Lisa Lepak
Suamico, WI

We have a house nestled in the woods in the country so our children, Mitchell and Maria, are lucky to experience the beauty of nature and the little animals it brings into our yard. Several years ago we decided to put up an extra Christmas tree for our animal friends. It's decorated with white lights and edible ornaments, such as dried apples, oranges, popcorn and a cranberry garland. An assortment of empty baskets is left under the tree along with a note to Santa asking him to fill the baskets with food for our animal friends. Sometimes Santa has brought dried corn for the squirrels and chipmunks, carrots for the bunnies, birdseed bells for the birds, dog biscuits for our dog and apples for the horses. The kids are always so excited to see what Santa brought for the animals, that they run to the nature tree first thing Christmas morning.

Share favorite family recipes with a dear friend...such a simple gift will mean a great deal to her.

Sheila Dye
Ada, OH

Our traditional holiday game begins early in fall. Each member of our family picks a snow date...everyone trying to guess when we will get the first snow that covers the ground. One rule: no cheating by watching the weather channel ahead of time! Next, we all choose our favorite home-cooked meal. Choices vary from barbecue ribs to a huge pan of lasagna; however, as Mom, if I win, we get to go out to my favorite restaurant! With the addition of in-laws and lots of grandchildren, our family continues to grow and so does the excitement of the game for all of us.

Cynthia Stricklan
Appleton, NY

When my daughter left home for college I missed her dearly, this was especially true for the holidays. We always planned our gifts, shopping and baking together and without her I was a bit depressed. It seemed all the excitement and anticipation was gone. Then, I thought of a new idea...I began celebrating the 12 days Christmas. I shopped for small little gifts that I thought would remind her of home and mailed one to her each day. On Christmas Eve, she would arrive home and I would give her the last present which was one she could add to her ornament collection. She loved receiving bits of Christmas from home, and it helped me get through the growing pains.

Sharing the Spirit

Lisa Lucas
Palmyra, VA

Around the second week in December, one of our group of friends hosts a "Greenery Party." Here's what we do: The hostess provides a large space, usually a barn, garage or basement, buckets of water for soaking florists' foam, hot and cold beverages, forks, cups, plates, bowls and napkins. Each person participating brings enough fresh greenery, holly, magnolia leaves and juniper berries for themselves and to share. We also bring the supplies we'll need to make a wreath, for example florist's foam, T-pins, ribbon, wire and wreath forms. We then spend the day making wreaths or swags to keep and give as gifts. Everyone packs a bag lunch, brings a holiday sweet with recipe to share and truly enjoys the holiday spirit. Not only do we visit, we share ideas on arrangements, decorations, recipes and gifts. It's a great way to start the season and before we leave, we've already decided who will host the party next year!

If you have friends who live far away, gather together your family, hold up a big sign that says "Merry Christmas!", take a picture and mail it to them...they'll love it!

Julie Penny
Highlands Ranch, CO

A few years ago, during the Holiday season, my family and I found ourselves "between churches" and with no place to worship on Christmas Eve. So my husband and I planned our own service to be held in our home. We designed a simple program sheet that was given to our parents, grandparents and siblings as they arrived. In it was included scripture readings, hymns and a time to share special memories of Christmas's past. Everyone had a part to read, so it was truly a personal experience for all involved. We ended our very special service, by singing Silent Night on our front porch under the softly falling snow…it was a magical evening!

Place a tiny potted cedar tree at each guest's place setting…a gift that will be remembered for many years to come.

100

Sharing the Spirit

Phyllis Peters
Three Rivers, MI

As a child, I longed for the winter months to arrive in our small Michigan village of White Pigeon. Our neighbors owned and operated a store three blocks from my home and they also owned an apple orchard just over the state line in Indiana. Each fall the family loaded ripe apples into crates then on a farm wagon that delivered them to a barn next to our property for winter storage. My brothers, sister and I loved to accept an invitation to spend an evening at the Lambert's house for apples and popcorn. The aroma of the popped corn and the large, wooden bowl of crunchy apples, so bright red and shiny were a special treat. We played games on a round, kitchen table covered with a red and white checked oilcloth. It was so simple, filled with fun and always a favorite way to spend a wintry evening.

What are your favorite things to do during Christmas?
"Open presents and be with my family...it's fun to be together as family."

Sarah, age 7

Marsha Kiss
Marysville, OH

Living in the country we don't see all the hustle and bustle of the holidays as our city friends do. So, I like to make the holidays extra special for my long-time neighbors. One of my favorite things to do on Christmas Eve afternoon is fill a large basket with all of the goodies I have made for our neighbors then go house to house and drop off their gifts without them seeing me. I usually leave my house about 1:30 in the afternoon, then go from home to home. The treats are wrapped up neatly, then placed in a red or green plastic bag tied with a bow in case it starts to snow. I leave them on the back step and go to visit the next home. In between visits I crank up the Christmas tunes on my car radio and it really gets me into the true spirit of the season, it really is better to give than to receive. I find my older neighbors absolutely love the surprise, so I try to make each gift special for their family. I keep a journal with the gifts I've given from year to year so that I don't repeat the same gifts the following year.

The best gifts are tied with heartstrings.

-Unknown

Sharing the Spirit

Sharon Myers
Littlestown, PA

When I think of my family's holiday traditions, it's not opening gifts on Christmas Eve, sitting on Santa's lap or singing carols by the fireplace. What I remember best is our family waking up on Christmas morning. It was a morning filled with laughter, the smell of my Grandfather's freshly-brewed coffee, hugs and kisses. We'd all rush in the living room with amazement in our eyes to see our tree lit up and surrounded by wonderful presents…we all wondered which ones were ours. But before we could open our gifts, we would listen as my Grandfather read from the Bible. At first it was hard to concentrate, seeing all those presents, but he captured our attention as he read and we listened closely. Those days are long gone and I'm a mom now with 3 children of my own; however one thing remains in my heart and mind still…our family has been and will always be filled with love for one another.

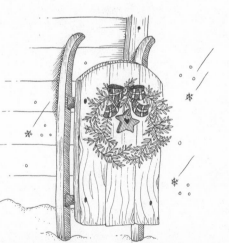

How does Santa leave presents if you don't have a chimney?
"He magically makes himself smaller and he goes through the cracks in the door."

Brooke, age 8

Nicole Anderson
Warren, OH

Christmas is a very special time of year for my family. For two complete days, we get to spend almost every waking moment together. This past Christmas we received the best Christmas present ever. Over the years my Grandmother had been keeping a journal of our Christmas celebrations. She wrote down what we ate, what went on, what time Santa Claus arrived and even that special toy all the children loved. This past Christmas each family received a personal copy of our memories...so many things happened that we had almost forgotten. We were so thrilled by this sweet book of memories and will continue to add to it each year.

Ask your grandparents to tell you about Christmas as it was while they were growing up...bring along a tape recorder and save their precious memories for your own children.

Sharing the Spirit

Janice Leffew
Seattle, WA

The sweet-tart aroma of a tangerine takes me back to my first grade classroom...there I took part in my first Christmas program. Our class was only a small part of that year's event, but to us it seemed like a huge part, we were excited and terrified! We practiced long and hard, both at school and at home. Finally the day for the program came. We were unusually quiet as 28 first graders dressed in flannel pajamas, prepared to march single file to the stage. We stood silently as the music teacher played a chord on the piano, then picked up the note and started to sing. We finished the song to thunderous applause...we had survived! Soon the auditorium filled with the sounds of sleigh bells and Santa arrived, handing out stockings filled with chocolates, candy canes, ribbon candy and a tangerine...this was my very first tangerine. Now every year I eagerly await the arrival of tangerines at my local grocery store because for me, this announces the start of the holiday season. As I place a bowl filled with tangerines on my Christmas table, I'm reminded of that little girl in pigtails who sang in her first Christmas program years ago.

When Santa & Mrs. Claus take a vacation, where do they go?
"Go to see their cousins. They like to stay with them inside and watch television."

Zachary, age 5

Christie Paul
Greenfield, IN

Ever since I can remember I have always been the first to wake up on Christmas morning. Before I woke everyone else up, I would take a few minutes to go and just look at the tree and smell the fragrant greenery. I'd reflect on the ornaments…each one had special meaning, either handmade or given to us as sentimental gifts. Sometimes I'd lay next to the tree and enjoy the twinkling lights and quietness…then I would take a deep breath and yell, "Wake up! It's Christmas!"

Cassandra Koerner
Middletown, NJ

When I was little we always had a great tall Christmas tree decorated with hundreds of little white lights. Every night I would lay down on the floor beside the tree and slide myself under it. I would stare up at the tree lights, pretend that they were stars and drift off to sleep. Twenty years later, I'm still falling asleep under my "stars."

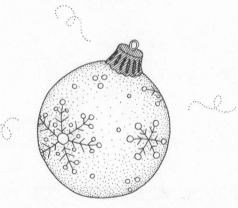

This year camp out under the Christmas tree…the kids will love it! Turn off all other lights and enjoy sleeping under the magical "stars".

106

Sharing the Spirit

Sandee Palumbo
Bonita, CA

For several years we've invited family & friends to join us for a "Night Before Christmas" party on Christmas Eve. Frosty the Snowman, our 30 year-old son, greets our guests at the door and soon we're all enjoying hearty soups and sandwiches, while the children stand watch at the front door looking for Santa. When Santa magically arrives, the children joyfully escort him to a rocking chair in front of the Christmas tree. Our most memorable gathering; however, was the year of the Persian Gulf War. When the call came that my nephew, who was stationed in Germany, would be leaving for Saudi Arabia on Christmas Eve, we were all heartbroken. He would be leaving behind his wife, who was expecting, and their 3 year-old daughter for the holidays. Soon though, we had a plan, we'd bring his wife and little girl to stay with us for Christmas and within 24 hours they were on their way! We wanted to surprise the entire family, so we "wrapped" them in a large box before everyone arrived. The party began as in years past and the setting was complete...Santa settled in his rocking chair and the sounds of Christmas music, but this year there was a very large gift by the tree. Soon the rustling of paper was heard and the "present" jumped out of the box! There wasn't a dry eye in the room, it truly was the meaning of Christmas.

Mary Jane Gaines
Lawrenceburg, KY

Every year my younger sister and I looked forward to Santa's visit at church the Sunday evening before Christmas. We'd eagerly wait as he handed out presents and when it was our turn, I felt he was always especially warm toward me and my sister. I remember telling my mother that Santa loved us more than the other children, but she would always say, "Santa loves all children." Then one year, I noticed Dad wasn't with us, but Mom reassured me he was sitting in the back with the rest of the fathers. When Santa handed me my gift, along with a big bear hug and a laugh, he seemed so familiar. I noticed his hands were identical to Dad's…a mechanic's hands are very identifiable. I asked Mom if Santa was a mechanic, like Dad, and I remember her telling me that Santa always made toys at Christmas so yes, he was sort of a mechanic. All evening long I sat there watching every move Santa made, almost forgetting to open my gift. The similarities were unbelievable…his hands, his voice, his laugh. Well, soon and without a doubt, I knew who Santa was. Many years later, I still believe in Santa. He was a jolly, sincere, hardworking man who taught me how to enjoy life to it's fullest and most importantly, how to laugh. Santa will always hold a special place in my heart.

How do Santa & Mrs. Claus decorate their home?
"Reindeer, lights, wreaths with red bows."
Ryan, age 6

Sharing the Spirit

Michelle Blunt
Burney, CA

As a young girl I lived in a very mild climate and because winter was always warm, the ice cream man came year 'round. To our delight, each holiday season Mom bought snow balls from him…delicious ice cream balls rolled in coconut. Each had a sprig of holly and a candle on top. We all eagerly anticipated this little bit of snow which we saved until Christmas Eve. With all the lights off, Mom would light the candles…I can still feel their warm glow. I haven't seen those magical ice cream treats since I was a kid, so now I make them for my children, it's still just as special.

Kim Smith
Broadview Heights, OH

We have a fun tradition of leaving large, quilted stockings on our kitchen table on Christmas Eve. Each Christmas morning when my husband lets the dog out, he just happens to find our stockings completely filled and chilled in the garage. Each stocking holds a small box of cereal, little cartons of milk and juice, a banana, a colorful disposable bowl, plate, spoon and napkin, small donuts or a muffin and a packet of hot cocoa. Our Christmas is a little less hectic and we have more time for opening gifts and playing with the children.

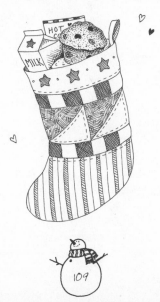

Irene Gobel
Spanaway, WA

Years ago our family began receiving "visits" from a Christmas elf...he's just 4 inches tall and is dressed in a red robe and jolly hat. On the first of December, he "magically" appears somewhere in our home. Each night he moves to a new location until finally Christmas morning he can be found on our tree. Then, the day after Christmas, he's gone for another year. What fun it is for our family to search for him each day...it wouldn't be Christmas without him.

Kathy Larsen
San Diego, CA

Each Christmas Eve, after our girls are asleep, I put on some cherry red lipstick and give them each a kiss on the forehead. When they wake up Christmas morning, they find Santa's kiss. Each one then spends the day seeing whose kiss will last the longest!

Children grow up way too fast...enjoy your family traditions and make some new ones. Take lots of pictures, hold hands, sing, laugh and make every Christmas one to remember.

Sharing the Spirit

Mary Lou Lieb
Bath, PA

We began this family tradition when our children were still small. Two weeks before Christmas we'd form an assembly line to make and bake cookies. I begin rolling out the dough, cutting out shapes and filling trays with cookies. The kids would decorate cookies however they liked, then pass them on to Dad for the final stage of baking these whimsical masterpieces. Needless to say, several cookies were always eaten by the time the next round began...they had to be tested! Together we've enjoyed this special day for 25 years and now that our daughter is married, we set aside a special day to reminisce, bake cookies and leave with a smiling face and a full tummy!

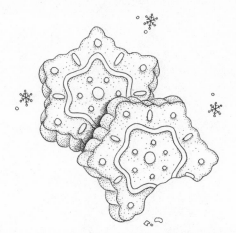

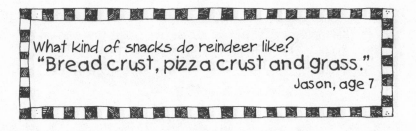

What kind of snacks do reindeer like?
"Bread crust, pizza crust and grass."
Jason, age 7

Rebecca Chrisman
Cirtus Heights, CA

One Christmas Eve I spent the day helping my 2 year-old great niece decorate gingerbread cookies. By the time the day was over, she had more icing on herself than on the cookies! I tried to keep out of the way, but I was covered with icing, too. We had a wonderful time. We took lots of pictures that day, had them developed and tucked them in a photo album. We also wrapped the decorated cookies and put both under the tree as a surprise for her parents. When we opened presents together, she couldn't wait to give her mom and dad their surprise. What a fun day and a memory I will always treasure.

What do the reindeer & elves do after Christmas is over?
"Take the lights and Christmas trees down. Maybe they could take a nap because of all the stuff they did."

Tyler, age 5

Sharing the Spirit

Kathy Fox
Easton, MD

Early in December I get together with a group of 10 to 15 good friends for an ornament exchange and holiday potluck. Everyone brings a handmade ornament and a tasty dish to share, along with the recipe. It's a wonderful afternoon as we sit around a toasty fire to exchange ornaments, enjoy delicious food and chat about our holiday plans. When the day's over, everyone goes home with several handmade ornaments, new recipes to try and the spirit of Christmas in their hearts.

Forth to the wood did merry men go,
to gather in the mistletoe.

-Sir Walter Scott

Melody Nicoll
La Crescenta, CA

What a wonderful childhood I had growing up in a small village in Wisconsin. One of my fondest memories is of Christmas Eve. Each child in our Sunday School had a little poem to memorize and recite during our Christmas Eve service and I wanted to help my younger sister memorize her poem…"Blessed Redeemer, we kneel at Thy feet, And ask Thee to keep us all blessed and sweet." When Mother came home I so proudly had my sister recite what I had taught her. Even now I can remember my embarrassment. At my young age, I wasn't familiar with the word "Redeemer," and had taught her to say "Blessed reindeer!"

What do the reindeer & elves do after Christmas is over?
"The elves find more reindeer to train for the next Christmas."

Kelli, age 6

114

Sharing the Spirit

Jean Sanders
Natchez, MS

Each year at Christmas time I choose something that reminds me of my granddaughter, Morghan. It could be a happy little ladybug ornament, because ladybugs are her favorite, or a reminder of something we did together during the year. I wrap up her gift and then write a letter to her about it as well as share with her all the joy she brings to my life. I seal up the letter, tape it to the package and tuck it in a safe place. Then, one day, she will receive these gifts when she marries or is on her own. I hope these letters will be a happy way for her to remember our time together and some of the highlights of her childhood.

Give your greeting cards a fun postmark! Address and put stamps on each, then place them in a large envelope and mail to the postmaster at: North Pole, Alaska, 99705, Santa Claus, Indiana 47579 or Christmas, Florida 32709. They'll postmark your cards, then mail them!

Candy Hannigan
Monument, CO

During the 26 years my husband was in the Air Force, we made so many good friends in all the places we lived and visited. To keep in touch with them, and our family, for the past 18 years we've mailed a Christmas ornament along with our family letter. Each year it's a fun challenge to create a new design, it has to be flat to mail easily, and although some years I worry I can't find a new idea, we always do. For example one year it was a red flannel mitten with a feather tree stitched on the front. When we visit friends during the holidays, it's great fun to see our past ornaments hanging on their trees. So many souvenirs get lost or are no longer used, but these ornaments bring back such wonderful memories of the places we've visited and the people we've known. This is one of my favorite traditions because it helps bring our family and friends together...even though we can't all be together.

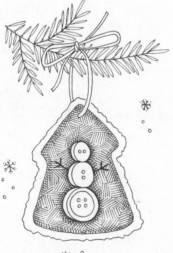

What kind of snacks do reindeer like?
"Apples, berries and hay."
Nikki, age 5

Sharing the Spirit

Bev Clock
Exeter, NH

When our children were very young, counting down the days to Christmas was simple using paper chains and Advent calendars. As they grew; however, it became harder. After much thought, we all agreed that it would be fun if each of us was a secret Santa. My husband gave a groan, but decided to play along "for the kids"...even though he's the biggest kid of all! We drew names at Thanksgiving so everyone would have plenty of time to make their surprises. During the weeks counting down to Christmas, we'd often see a light coming from under someone's door. Although nothing was said, I'm sure each of us was wondering if a special something was being made just for us...the fun was in the secrecy! Delivery of our gifts is 5 days before Christmas and the final gift is given Christmas Eve. Even though our children are now in their 20's, we still enjoy this family tradition...it's a sweet time when we can all be together.

White lunch bags are just the right size for holding little surprises. Use paint or markers to turn them into cheerful snowmen and top off each with a child-size knit cap...so cute!

Linda Charles
Delafield, WI

Our whole family has always looked forward to Christmas, but my favorite memories are of those when I was young. Christmas morning as we opened our presents, suddenly, we'd hear jingle bells. Jumping to our feet, we looked out the window only to find Santa at our door! He'd come inside and warm up, then pass out gifts...parents, as well as kids, loved these early morning visits. It wasn't until I was a little older I realized Santa was our neighbor and then, many years later, we we were saddened to hear our Santa passed away. A few weeks before Christmas; however, I heard that his son was now taking over as Santa Claus and I asked if he could visit our home on Christmas Eve. That night, while we were all opening presents, my 2 year-old son heard jingle bells. He ran excitedly to the window, but when Santa came in the front door he was a little nervous and began to cry. We invited Santa in, reassured my son that all was fine and had a wonderful time talking and laughing. All too soon Santa had to leave and my son began to cry again...this time, because he wanted him to stay, we all did.

Ah friends, dear friends, as years go on and heads get gray, how fast the guests do go! Touch hands, touch hands, with those who stay...around the Christmas board touch hands.

-Wm. H. H. Murray

Sharing the Spirit

LauraLee Chambers
Ossining, NY

Christmas is an extra special time to collect memories for my baby daughter. On her first Christmas, at 6 months old, we invited loved ones over for her first holiday gathering. Each guest was asked to bring an ornament to start her collection. I displayed them across our mantel so we could admire them, then at the end of the season I began an ornament journal just for her. I sketched or photographed each ornament on a page in her book and recorded the year, name of the person who gave it to her, as well as any special information. I have a journal of my own and love looking back to see how each one became a part of our beautiful collection. I know she will, too.

Marianne Lukas
East Islip, NY

When our family comes together for Christmas dinner, we put a large, round candle in the middle of the table to represent all our loved ones that can't be with us during this special time. As we sit down to dinner, we light the candle, say a prayer and enjoy it's warm glow through dinner and dessert.

A Christmas to Remember

Transfer sentimental family photos on fabric and create a memory quilt...what a thoughtful gift.

Dust off your camera and camcorder...capture every special moment! Kids making snow angels or posing in their new jammies and Grandpa sneaking a kiss from Grandma under the mistletoe will be such sweet remembrances.

On a frosty day, let your little ones snuggle in bed with you. Keep a basket of favorite Christmas books near the bed to read together.

Share special gifts...a dainty teacup that belonged to Grandma or a cookbook with her handwritten notes in the margin, will be a welcome and cherished gift.

Bundle everyone up and go caroling, take flowers to a nursing home and make a wish on a shooting star, come home to chocolatey cocoa and popcorn.

Christmas Morning Delights

Breakfast & Brunch to beGIN your Special day.

Baked Apple Donuts

Joanna Scoresby
Mount Vernon, OH

They're not really donuts...they're wonderful, tender muffins.

1-1/2 c. all-purpose flour
1-3/4 t. baking powder
1/2 t. salt
1/2 t. nutmeg
1/2 c. sugar

1/2 c. shortening
1 egg, beaten
1/4 c. milk
1 c. apples, peeled and grated

Sift together flour, baking powder, salt, nutmeg and sugar; cut in shortening until mixture is fine. Combine egg, milk and apples. Add to dry ingredients; mix quickly. Fill greased muffin tins 3/4 full and bake at 350 degrees for 20 to 30 minutes. Remove from pan and roll in prepared topping. Makes 12 servings.

Topping:

1/2 c. butter, melted
1/2 c. sugar

1 t. cinnamon

Stir together all ingredients until well blended. Roll warm muffins in butter mixture and set on wax paper to cool slightly.

Cover a kitchen tree with nothing but
cookies...reindeer, gingerbread men,
snowflakes and stars.

Christmas Morning

Ooey-Gooey Pancake S'mores

Keli Morris
Sacramento, CA

Both kids and adults love these chocolatey pancakes!

2 c. biscuit baking mix
1-1/3 c. milk
2 T. sugar
1 t. vanilla extract
1 egg
1/2 c. graham crackers,
   crumbled, divided

14 T. marshmallow creme,
   divided
14 T. chocolate chips, divided
Garnish: graham crackers,
   crumbled and chocolate chips

Stir together biscuit baking mix, milk, sugar, vanilla and egg; pour a little less than 1/4 cup onto a hot, oiled griddle. Cook until bubbles begin to form around the edges of the pancakes. Sprinkle about one tablespoon graham cracker crumbs over each pancake and turn them over. Cook until golden and remove from griddle; spread one tablespoon marshmallow creme over the crumb side of each pancake, then sprinkle one tablespoon chocolate chips over marshmallow creme. Top with an additional pancake and spread an additional tablespoon of marshmallow creme over. Garnish with graham cracker crumbs and chocolate chips over top. Makes 6 to 8 servings.

Enjoy an early morning breakfast by the glow of candlelight...attach a miniature candle clip to the side of each plate.

Caramel Apple Pudding

Robbin Chamberlain
Worthington, OH

When our family gathers for a holiday breakfast, my sister, Deb, is always asked to bring this. It's delicious with anything you've planned for breakfast or brunch.

2 c. green apple, sliced
1/4 c. water
3/4 t. cinnamon
1/2 c. brown sugar, packed
2 T. corn syrup
2 T. margarine
1/4 c. pecan pieces

3 eggs, beaten
1-1/4 c. milk
1 t. vanilla extract
1/4 t. nutmeg
8 to 10 thick slices Italian bread, divided

Combine apple and water in a saucepan; bring to a boil, then reduce heat. Cook, covered, over low heat for 5 to 7 minutes or until apples are tender; stirring occasionally. Drain in a colander and transfer apples to a small mixing bowl. Gently stir cinnamon into apples; set aside. In the same small saucepan, combine brown sugar, corn syrup and margarine. Cook and stir over medium heat until mixture comes to a boil; remove from heat. Pour mixture into a greased 9"x9" baking dish; sprinkle pecans on top. Whisk together eggs, milk, vanilla and nutmeg; set aside. Arrange half of bread slices in the baking dish over caramel mixture, trimming bread to fit. Spoon apples evenly over bread layer. Arrange remaining bread slices on top. Carefully pour the egg mixture over bread pressing the bread down gently to moisten the slices completely. Cover with plastic wrap and refrigerate for at least 3 hours. Before baking, remove plastic wrap. Bake, uncovered, at 325 degrees for 40 to 45 minutes or until a knife inserted comes out clean. Remove from oven; run a knife around the edges to loosen and let stand for 15 minutes. Carefully invert pudding onto a platter. Spoon any remaining caramel mixture over pudding. Cut into wedges; serve warm or cool. Makes 8 servings.

Christmas Morning

Old-Fashioned Blueberry Muffins

Kristyn Stephens
Bruceville, IN

Start your day with these and a cup of chamomile tea.

3 c. all-purpose flour, divided	1 egg
4 t. baking powder	1 c. milk
1/2 t. salt	1 t. vanilla extract
1 c. sugar, divided	1-1/2 c. blueberries
1/2 c. butter, divided	1/2 t. cinnamon

Stir together 2-1/2 cups flour, baking powder and salt; set aside.
Cream together 1/2 cup sugar, 1/4 cup butter and egg; combine with
flour mixture until crumbly. Add milk and vanilla; mix until blended.
Fold in blueberries and spoon into lightly greased muffin tins
2/3 full. Combine remaining sugar, flour and cinnamon and cut in
remaining butter until crumbly. Sprinkle topping over the batter. Bake,
uncovered, at 375 degrees for 20 to 30 minutes. Makes 12 servings.

What do the reindeer & elves do after Christmas
is over?

"Sleep!"

Sarah, age 7

Baked Eggs

Gloria Kaufmann
Orrville, OH

These would also be delicious spooned over English muffins.

4 T. butter
1 onion, diced
1/4 c. all-purpose flour
2 c. hot milk
1 c. cooked ham, diced

6 eggs, hard-boiled and diced
1/2 c. shredded Swiss cheese
2 T. bread crumbs
paprika to taste

Heat butter and onion in a skillet; stir in flour. Remove from heat and add milk, stirring rapidly until smooth. Return to heat and cook until boiling. Arrange ham and eggs in an ungreased 13"x9" baking dish. Pour milk mixture over ham and eggs, sprinkle on cheese, bread crumbs and paprika. Bake, uncovered, at 375 degrees for 12 to 15 minutes or until cheese is bubbly. Makes 10 servings.

There are dozens of clever uses for your button collection...stitch them on the cuff of a stocking, around the edges of napkins or string lots together for a homespun garland.

Christmas Morning

Christmas Morn Casserole

Kelly Hoefer
Bellevue, NE

*Ready to bake in only 15 minutes, so you can get back
to all the Christmas morning fun!*

20-oz. pkg. frozen hash browns,
 thawed
4 c. shredded Monterey Jack
 cheese
2 c. cooked ham, diced

7 eggs
1 c. milk
1/2 t. salt
1/2 t. ground mustard

Place hash browns in a greased 13"x9" baking dish. Sprinkle with
cheese and ham; set aside. Beat eggs, milk, salt and mustard together;
pour over ham. Bake, covered, at 350 degrees for one hour. Uncover
and bake an additional 15 minutes or until golden. Makes 8 servings.

What do the reindeer & elves do after Christmas
is over?
"They lay down and take a nap. Especially
the reindeer because they are worn out."

Austin, age 4

Sausage-Filled Crêpes

Renae Reu
Luverne, MN

Enjoy with a tall glass of freshly squeezed orange juice!

3 eggs, beaten
1 c. milk
1 T. oil
1 c. all-purpose flour
1/2 t. salt
1 lb. ground sausage, browned

1/4 c. onion, diced
1-1/2 c. pasteurized process
    cheese spread, shredded
3-oz. pkg. cream cheese
1/2 c. sour cream
1/4 c. butter

Whisk together eggs, milk and oil. Stir in flour and salt; mixing well. Lightly grease a 5" or 7" skillet and place on medium-high heat. Using a ladle or small cup, spoon in about 2 tablespoons of batter, then quickly tilt the pan to coat the bottom. The batter should be in a thin layer. Cook for 3 to 4 minutes, or until the edges are golden and lift up easily. Turn it with a spatula and cook the second side, for only 3 to 4 minutes. Place crêpe on a plate, cover to keep warm and repeat with remaining batter. Combine sausage, onion, cheese and cream cheese until well blended. Place 2 tablespoons of sausage mixture down the center of each crêpe, roll up and place in a greased 13"x9" baking dish. Bake, covered, at 375 degrees for 40 minutes. In a small mixing bowl, combine sour cream and butter; spoon over crêpes. Uncover and bake an additional 5 minutes. Makes 8 servings.

Christmas Morning

Country Breakfast Skillet

Natalie Roberge
Stillwater, MN

All of your early morning favorites together!

16-oz. pkg. frozen hash browns, thawed
salt and pepper to taste
garlic powder to taste
6 to 8 eggs
1/3 c. milk

1 to 2 tomatoes, chopped
4 to 6 green onions, thinly sliced
1/4 lb. thinly sliced, cooked ham, chopped
1-1/2 c. shredded Cheddar cheese

Cook hash browns according to package skillet directions; season with salt, pepper and garlic powder; set aside. Beat eggs with milk; add tomatoes, onions and ham. Stir egg mixture into hash browns, and over medium heat, stir quickly to scramble. As the eggs begin to firm, add cheese and continue to stir until eggs are cooked and set. Makes 4 servings.

You can make beautiful gift tags by slipping a single photograph or pressed flowers into a clear envelope.

Petite Breakfast Tarts

Susan Young
Madison, AL

So quick to prepare...I make them while my son naps!

1 c. all-purpose flour	3/4 c. brown sugar, packed
1/2 c. butter	1 egg
3-oz. pkg. cream cheese, softened	1 t. vanilla extract
	1 T. butter, softened
1 c. pecans, finely chopped	

Place flour in a medium mixing bowl, cut in butter and cream cheese with pastry blender or 2 knives; chill dough for one hour. Shape dough into one-inch balls and press in lightly oiled small tart pans or mini muffin tins. Sprinkle one tablespoon chopped pecans into each dough-lined tart pan. Stir together brown sugar, egg, vanilla and one tablespoon butter; spoon mixture over pecans in each tin. Fill each tin slightly less than half full. Bake at 350 degrees for 20 minutes. Mixture will be puffy with a golden crust on the edges. Makes approximately 1-1/2 to 2 dozen.

Leave your neighbor a morning surprise. Paint a snowman face on a round box, then fill with lots of goodies for a quick & easy breakfast...muffin mixes, gourmet coffees and homemade preserves.

Christmas Morning

Brunch Croissants

Donna Vogel
The Colony, TX

I like to top these with sour cream and salsa.

1-1/2 c. cooked ham, cubed
8-oz. pkg. cream cheese

12-oz. tube refrigerated
croissants

In a medium mixing bowl, combine ham and cream cheese. Unroll and separate croissants; place a dollop of ham mixture on each croissant. Roll up and place on an ungreased baking sheet. Bake, uncovered, at 425 degrees for 15 to 18 minutes. Makes 8 servings.

Best Frittata

Judy Borecky
Escondido, CA

Cut in squares and served with fresh fruit, this makes a wonderful light brunch for overnight guests.

1/2 c. margarine, melted
10 eggs, beaten
1 lb. shredded Monterey Jack
    cheese
1 lb. cottage cheese
6-oz. jar marinated artichoke
    hearts, puréed

7-oz. can diced green chilies,
    drained
1 t. baking powder
1/2 t. salt

Thoroughly combine all ingredients and pour onto an ungreased 15"x10" baking sheet with one-inch sides. Bake, uncovered, at 350 degrees for 30 to 35 minutes or until tests done; cut in squares. Makes 10 servings.

Invite friends over for brunch before a day of shopping...a terrific way to start the day!

Cinnamon Swirls

Judy Jenkins
Knoxville, TN

Best warm from the oven with an icy glass of milk.

8-oz. tube refrigerated crescent
   rolls
2 T. margarine, softened
1/2 t. cinnamon
1-1/2 t. sugar

1/4 c. chopped walnuts
1/3 c. powdered sugar
1 t. milk
1/4 t. vanilla extract

Unroll crescent roll dough and separate in 4 rectangles. Press seams
to seal; spread margarine over dough. Mix together cinnamon and
sugar and sprinkle evenly over rectangles. Press walnuts into
cinnamon-sugar mixture. Roll up jelly roll-style, starting with long
side; press edges to seal. Cut each log into 5 slices. Place into a lightly
greased 8" round cake pan. Bake, uncovered, at 350 degrees for
12 minutes or until golden on top. Combine powdered sugar, milk and
vanilla, stirring until smooth and drizzle over warm rolls.
Makes 20 rolls.

How does Santa leave presents if you don't have a chimney?
**"Go through the front door, and he can
without keys because he's magic."**
Zachary, age 5

Christmas Morning

Amish Baked Oatmeal

Lynda McCormick
Burkburnett, TX

For me, this is one of those warm, homestyle dishes that hits the spot on a cold, wintry morning. I love it topped with homemade applesauce and sprinkled with cinnamon and nutmeg...yummy!

1-1/2 c. quick-cooking oats,
   uncooked
1/2 c. brown sugar, packed
1/2 c. milk
1/4 c. butter, melted

1 egg
1 t. baking powder
3/4 t. fine sea salt
1 t. vanilla extract
Garnish: warm milk

Stir together oats, brown sugar, milk, butter, egg, baking powder, salt and vanilla. Spread evenly into a greased 13"x9" baking dish. Bake, uncovered, at 350 degrees for 25 to 30 minutes or until edges are golden. Immediately spoon into individual serving bowls and pour milk over. Makes 6 servings.

A charming placecard...slip a round ornament in a foil baking cup, attach the name card to the hanger.

133

Caramel French Toast

Leah Lizun
Denville, NJ

Serve with a side of crispy bacon...oh, so wonderful!

1/2 c. butter	6 eggs
1 c. brown sugar, packed	1-1/2 c. milk
2 T. corn syrup	2 t. vanilla extract
1 loaf French bread, cubed	cinnamon to taste

Blend together butter, brown sugar and corn syrup in a medium saucepan. Bring to a boil over medium heat, then remove from heat. Pour into a ungreased 13"x9" baking dish. Place bread in baking dish over sauce. Whisk together eggs, milk and vanilla until well blended; pour over bread and sprinkle with cinnamon. Bake, uncovered, at 300 degrees for one hour. Makes 8 servings.

Bells are magical...wire different sizes on a wreath, string several on ribbon and hang from your doorknob, tie one on the cat's collar or the baby's booties!

134

Christmas Morning

Cinnamon-Sugar Donuts

Joann Uecker
Redmond, WA

*I started making these years ago as a Girl Scout leader, now my
daughters and I love to make them together.*

2 T. oil
7-1/2 oz. tube refrigerated
    biscuits

cinnamon to taste
sugar to taste

Add oil to a large skillet over medium-high heat. Cut each biscuit into
fourths and add several to hot oil, cooking until golden. Drain on
paper towels; repeat with remaining biscuits. Combine cinnamon and
sugar in a small mixing bowl, roll donuts in cinnamon-sugar mixture.
Makes approximately 2-1/2 dozen.

Crullers

Wendy Paffenroth
Pine Island, NY

These are the kind you could only find at the local diner years ago.

2 T. butter
1 c. sugar
2 eggs, beaten
4 c. all-purpose flour
3-1/2 t. baking powder

1/2 t. nutmeg
1/2 t. salt
1 c. whipping cream
Garnish: powdered sugar

Cream butter and sugar; add eggs and beat until well blended. Sift the
dry ingredients together; add alternately with cream to sugar mixture.
Mix until a soft dough forms and place on a floured surface. Pat lightly
until just thick enough to cut into 24, 1/2-inch wide strips. Bring the
ends together and twist them like a corkscrew. Using a heavy pot and
a candy thermometer, add enough oil to equal 4 inches. When oil
reaches 360 degrees, add crullers, one at a time. When golden, turn.
Repeat with remaining batter. Drain on a brown paper grocery bag;
place on a platter and dust with powdered sugar. Makes about
2 dozen.

135

Cream Cheese Danish

Kay Datz
Chattanooga, TN

You'll need to make several batches...they go quickly!

2 8-oz. tubes refrigerated
   crescent rolls, divided
8-oz. plus 3-oz. pkg. cream
   cheese, softened
1 c. sugar

4 T. butter, melted
1 c. powdered sugar
1/2 t. vanilla extract
3 T. milk

Spread one tube of crescent rolls into the bottom of an ungreased
13"x9" baking dish. Cream together cream cheese and sugar; spread
over top of rolls. Top cream cheese mixture with the remaining tube of
crescent rolls; pour butter over all. Bake, uncovered, at 350 degrees for
25 to 30 minutes or until golden. In a small mixing bowl, combine
powdered sugar, vanilla and milk; drizzle over danish. Cut in squares.
Makes 14 servings.

A delightful centerpiece...tie ornaments on lengths of
ribbon, slip the ribbon though holes made in a canning jar
lid. Fill the jar with coarse salt and gently secure the lid.

Christmas Morning

Streusel Coffee Cake

Kim Maloney
Schaumburg, IL

Passed on from generation to generation, Grandma used to make this coffee cake as well as her mother before her. As it bakes, a heavenly aroma lingers throughout the house.

3/4 c. butter, divided
2-1/2 c. sugar, divided
2 eggs, separated and divided
1 t. vanilla extract
3-1/4 c. all-purpose flour,
    divided

4 t. baking powder
1 c. milk
1-1/2 T. cinnamon

Cream together 1/4 cup butter and 1-1/2 cups sugar; add egg yolks and vanilla. Beat egg whites together and add to butter mixture. Sift together 2-1/4 cups flour and baking powder, add to butter mixture and stir in milk gradually. Pour coffee cake into a greased 13"x9" baking dish. Bake, uncovered, at 350 degrees for 15 minutes. Combine remaining flour, sugar, butter and cinnamon until mixture becomes crumbly. Sprinkle topping onto cake and bake an additional 30 to 35 minutes or until center tests done. Makes 16 servings.

How do Santa & Mrs. Claus decorate their home?
"With little trees and snow angels."

Tyler, age 5

Cinnamon Rolls

Dawn Gilmore
Petoskey, MI

You could drizzle on a powdered sugar glaze if you'd like, but these sweet cinnamon rolls are so tasty, they really don't need it.

3/4 c. warm water
2 pkgs. active dry yeast
1/2 c. sugar
1 t. salt
2 eggs

1/2 c. shortening
1/2 c. plus 2 T. butter, divided
4 c. all-purpose flour
cinnamon-sugar to taste

Stir together water, yeast, sugar, salt, eggs, shortening, 1/2 cup butter and flour; knead about 5 minutes on a lightly floured board. Let rise in a lightly oiled bowl until double in size. Roll into a large rectangle until dough is 1/4-inch thick. Spread with remaining butter and sprinkle with cinnamon-sugar. Roll up jelly roll-style and cut into one-inch slices. Place slices on a greased baking sheet and bake, uncovered, at 350 degrees for 15 to 20 minutes or until golden. Makes 12 to 14 servings.

Chill December brings the sleet,
blazing fire and Christmas treat.

-Mother Goose

Christmas Morning

Sugar-Topped Muffins

Julie Paschen
Kentwood, MI

Nothing's better to wake up to on a chilly morning than warm muffins on the breakfast table.

18-1/4 oz. pkg. white cake mix
   with pudding
1/2 t. nutmeg
1 c. milk

2 eggs
1/3 c. sugar
1/2 t. cinnamon
1/4 c. butter, melted

Blend cake mix, nutmeg, milk and eggs on low speed until moistened; beat 2 minutes on high. Fill muffin tins lined with paper baking cups 2/3 full. Bake at 350 degrees for 15 to 25 minutes or until golden brown. Cool muffins for 5 minutes; remove from pan. Combine sugar and cinnamon in a small bowl. Immediately dip muffin tops in butter, then in sugar mixture. Serve warm. Makes 24 muffins.

What do the reindeer & elves do after Christmas is over?
"The reindeer fly south for the winter and the elves go on vacation with the Clauses."
Kyle & Sean, ages 6 and 3

Potato Snowflake Donuts

Judy Ann Bathrick
Wellsboro, PA

On the first snowfall of the year, our family gets together to make these...we have such wonderful fun!

2 c. sugar
4 t. baking powder
4 c. all-purpose flour
1-1/2 c. milk

1 c. hot mashed potatoes
2 T. butter
Garnish: powdered sugar

Stir together sugar, baking powder and flour; add milk and blend in potatoes and butter. Mix thoroughly, then roll out on a well floured board until 1/2-inch thick. Cut with round biscuit cutter; set aside. Add enough oil to a deep fryer or heavy pot to equal 4 inches. Heat to medium-high. A candy thermometer should read 360 degrees when oil is hot enough. Add donuts, 2 or 3 at a time, turning over until all sides are golden. Drain well on paper towels. Roll in powdered sugar if desired. Makes about 2 dozen.

Kids have done it for years and it's still as much fun today! Stencil snowflakes on your windows by dabbing water-soluble paint over doilies...when winter's over, they wipe right off with a damp sponge.

Christmas Morning

Baked French Toast

Tammy McCartney
Oxford, OH

Try a sampling of different syrups with this casserole...blueberry, strawberry, boysenberry or honey-maple.

10 oz. thinly sliced French bread
8 eggs
3 c. milk
4 t. sugar
3/4 t. salt
1 T. vanilla extract
2 T. margarine, cubed

Arrange bread slices in a greased 13"x9" baking dish. Beat eggs with milk, sugar, salt and vanilla. Pour over bread in baking dish. Cover with aluminum foil and refrigerate at least 4 hours. Uncover and dot with margarine. Bake, uncovered, at 350 degrees for 45 to 50 minutes or until bread is puffy and golden. Let stand for 5 minutes before serving. Makes 8 servings.

Best of all are the decorations the grandchildren have made...fat little stars and rather crooked Santas, shaped out of dough and baked in the oven.

–Gladys Taber

Hash Brown Quiche

*Barbara Cooper
Orion, IL*

Shared with me by a good friend, I like to serve this at bridal showers, family reunions and during the holidays.

3 c. frozen hash browns, thawed	2 eggs
1/3 c. margarine, melted	1/2 c. milk
1 c. cooked ham, diced	1/2 t. salt
1 c. shredded Cheddar cheese	1/4 t. pepper
1/4 c. green pepper, diced	

Press hash browns into the bottom and up the sides of an ungreased 9" pie plate; drizzle with margarine. Bake, uncovered, at 425 degrees for 25 minutes. Stir together ham, cheese and green pepper; spoon over hash browns. Beat eggs, milk, salt and pepper together; pour over top. Reduce heat to 350 degrees and bake an additional 25 to 30 minutes or until eggs are set. Allow to stand for 10 minutes before slicing. Makes 6 to 8 servings.

Treat guests to breakfast in bed!

Christmas Morning

Brunch Casserole

Sharon Cook
Madison, WV

Change a couple of ingredients and you have a whole new casserole...try using maple or sage-flavored sausage and Swiss or Co-Jack cheese...wonderful!

8-oz. tube crescent rolls
1 lb. ground sausage, browned
4 eggs

3/4 c. milk
salt and pepper to taste
2 c. shredded Cheddar cheese

Lightly oil a 15"x10" baking sheet with one-inch sides. Lay crescent rolls on baking sheet, pressing together to remove perforations. Place sausage evenly over rolls. Beat eggs, add milk, salt and pepper together; pour over sausage. Layer on cheese and bake, uncovered, at 425 degrees for 15 to 20 minutes or until golden. Makes 12 to 14 servings.

How does Santa leave presents if you don't have a chimney?
"Santa just finds a way...he's Santa!"
Sarah, age 7

Brown Sugar Apples

Kathy Grashoff
Fort Wayne, IN

Spoon over waffles or pancakes, or enjoy just by themselves!

1 lb. sliced bacon, diced
12 apples, cored and sliced

1 c. brown sugar, packed
1 T. cinnamon

Cook bacon until crisp; add apples, brown sugar and cinnamon. Stir over low heat until apples are tender. Makes 16 to 20 servings.

Morning Glory Muffins

Cheryl Sanborn
Swartz Creek, MI

Filled with carrots, coconut and apples...a great way to start the day.

1 c. all-purpose flour
1 c. whole-wheat flour
1-1/2 c. sugar
2 t. baking soda
1/2 t. salt
3 eggs, beaten

3/4 c. oil
2 t. vanilla extract
2 apples, cored and chopped
2 c. carrots, shredded
1/2 c. flaked coconut

Sift together flours, sugar, baking soda and salt; set aside. Combine remaining ingredients in a small mixing bowl; add to dry mixture and blend. Spoon batter 2/3 full into muffin tins coated with non-stick vegetable spray. Bake at 400 degrees for 18 minutes or until muffins test done in the center. Makes 12 muffins.

What's your favorite treat to leave Santa and why?
"Cheese because it has milk in it for Santa to make him strong so he can lift his bag of toys easier."
Ryan, age 6

Christmas Morning

Cheddar-Bacon Bites

Lynda McCormick
Burkburnett, TX

Heading out for a day of shopping? These are great for breakfast on the run!

2/3 c. butter, softened
2/3 c. sugar
1 egg
1 t. vanilla extract
3/4 c. all-purpose flour
1/2 t. baking soda
1/2 t. salt

6 slices bacon, crisply cooked
  and crumbled
1-1/4 c. oats, uncooked
1 c. shredded Cheddar cheese
1/2 c. honey-nut wheat germ

Cream together butter, sugar, egg and vanilla. Beat in flour, baking soda and salt; stir in remaining ingredients. Drop by rounded teaspoonfuls onto greased baking sheet; batter will spread. Bake at 350 degrees for 10 to 12 minutes. Makes 4 dozen.

Bits of vintage fabric add a special touch to handmade ornaments and stockings or tied around several recipe cards as a gift.

Warm Spiced Fruit

Peggy Frazier
Indianapolis, IN

One recipe I can truly say everyone loves.

20-oz. plus 8-oz. cans pineapple
    chunks, juice reserved
29-oz. can sliced peaches,
    drained
29-oz. can pear halves,
    quartered and drained

3/4 c. brown sugar, packed
1/4 c. butter
2 3-inch cinnamon sticks
1/2 t. ground ginger

Combine pineapple, peaches and pears; spoon into a 3-1/2 quart
baking dish. Blend together brown sugar, butter, cinnamon, ginger and
reserved pineapple juice in a saucepan; bring to a boil. Reduce heat
and simmer 5 minutes; discard cinnamon sticks. Pour over fruit and
bake, uncovered, at 350 degrees for 30 minutes or until heated
through. Makes 10 to 12 servings.

Fresh bagels and coffee delivered from the local
bakery each Saturday morning in December make a
a welcome and yummy gift!

Christmas Morning

Orange Streusel Coffee Cake

Vickie

You could easily substitute lemon juice and lemon zest in this recipe...it would be just as yummy!

2 c. plus 1/4 c. all-purpose flour,
   divided
1 t. salt
1 c. sugar, divided
2 t. baking powder
1 T. orange zest

1 egg, beaten
1/2 c. milk
1/2 c. orange juice
1/2 c. oil
2 T. butter

Combine 2 cups flour, salt, 1/2 cup sugar and baking powder; sift and stir in zest. Make a well in the center of the dry ingredients; set aside. Thoroughly blend egg, milk, orange juice and oil. Combine with flour mixture; batter will be lumpy. Pour in a greased 9" cake pan. Mix remaining flour, sugar and butter together; sprinkle evenly over cake. Bake at 375 degrees for 35 minutes or until center tests done. Makes 8 servings.

Why not get together with neighbors and have a potluck breakfast? Everyone brings their favorite dish...pancakes, sausage, French toast and you supply the coffee, tea, juice and cocoa...how fun!

Yuletide Spirit

Spend a wintry morning with your family...just being together.
Build a fire, sip creamy cocoa, enjoy the twinkling lights,
frosty windowpanes and stay in your jammies!

Once everyone's up, really enjoy a hearty breakfast. Sausage,
pancakes, real maple syrup, eggs, toast with lots of butter and
homemade preserves. Then bundle up and get everyone
outside...take a walk, build a snowman, make snow angels!

A holiday brunch can be your gift to friends and neighbors.
Make it a casual morning, invite guests to come when they can
and stay as long as they'd like. Keep the menu simple...slices
of quiche, muffins and fruit salad served with juice and
chamomile tea are wonderful ways to start the day.

Try something new for breakfast...add cranberry juice and
kiwi slices to ice cube trays and freeze...serve with tall
glasses of fresh orange juice. Add chocolate chips to
pancake batter or drizzle warm orange marmalade
over French toast. Layer all your favorites in one
bowl...scrambled eggs, crumbled bacon then
hashbrowns topped with sausage gravy!

OLD FASHIONED ROLLED OATS

Festive Feasting

Delicious Meals for your Family Gatherings.

Creamy Crabmeat Soup

Beth Ullman
Pomfret, MD

A creamy soup with a delicate taste.

1 cube vegetable bouillon
1 c. boiling water
1/4 c. onion, chopped
1/4 c. margarine
2 T. all-purpose flour
1 t. salt
1/4 t. celery salt

1/8 t. pepper
1 t. hot pepper sauce
2 c. milk
2 c. half-and-half
1 lb. flaked crabmeat
Garnish: fresh parsley, snipped

Dissolve bouillon in water; set aside. Sauté onion in margarine until tender. Blend in flour and seasonings. Gradually pour in milk, half-and-half and bouillon mixture; stir until thick enough to coat the back of a spoon. Add crabmeat; heat but do not boil. Garnish with parsley. Makes 6 servings.

Lay strings of battery operated white lights on your holiday table. They'll sparkle against your glasses and china...so lovely.

Festive Feasting

French Onion Soup

Karen Pilcher
Burleson, TX

Be sure to prepare this soup the night before you want to serve it...definitely worth the extra time.

1/4 c. plus 2 T. butter
1-1/4 lbs. onion, sliced
1 t. pepper
1 T. paprika
1 bay leaf
1/2 c. all-purpose flour

6 c. chicken broth, divided
1-1/2 t. salt
pepper to taste
Garnish: sliced French bread and
    sliced Swiss cheese

Melt butter in a stockpot, add onion and sauté slowly for 30 minutes. Stir in pepper, paprika, bay leaf, flour and one cup chicken broth. Let simmer for an additional 10 minutes, then add remaining broth and continue to simmer for 2 hours. Add salt and pepper to taste, stir and refrigerate overnight. When ready to serve, heat soup over low and remove bay leaf. Spoon into oven-proof bowls, top with a slice of French bread and a slice of cheese. Place under broiler 2 to 3 inches from heat source for 3 to 4 minutes or until cheese is melted. Makes 4 to 6 servings.

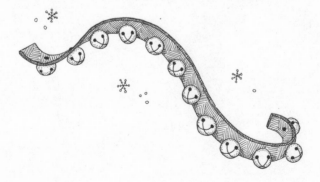

Jingle bells, jingle bells, jingle all the way!

–James Pierpont

Wild Rice Soup

Gail Saucier
Mankato, MN

For a special touch, top with crispy homemade croutons.

1 c. wild rice, uncooked
3 c. chicken broth
1 lb. sliced bacon, crisply cooked
    and crumbled, drippings
    reserved
1 onion, chopped
2 10-3/4 oz. cans cream of
    potato soup

2 4-oz. cans sliced mushrooms,
    undrained
2 c. half-and-half
5-oz. jar sharp pasteurized
    process cheese spread
2 c. water

Simmer rice in chicken broth until all liquid is absorbed; set aside.
Spoon bacon drippings in a saucepan, and sauté onion. Stir in bacon,
cream of potato soup, mushrooms, half-and-half, cheese, water and
rice. Heat, but don't boil. Makes 12 cups.

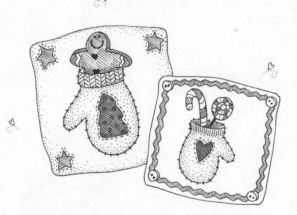

Stitch mitten pockets on pillows...what a clever gift idea!
Tuck candy canes, seed packets, recipe cards
or bags of herbal tea inside.

Festive Feasting

Creamy Asparagus Soup

Cathy Sackett
Sacramento, CA

A friend and I had asparagus soup for dinner at a local diner and liked it, but we agreed it could be better. I couldn't find a recipe in any of my cookbooks, so began experimenting...this one is the result of six different combinations; I think it's a winner!

32-oz. can chicken broth	salt and white pepper to taste
1 lb. asparagus, chopped	4 T. butter
1 T. lemon juice	4 T. all-purpose flour
1 onion, diced	1-1/2 c. half-and-half

Combine chicken broth, asparagus, lemon juice, onion, salt and pepper in a stockpot. Bring to a boil, reduce heat to low and cover. Continue to simmer for 8 to 10 minutes or until asparagus is tender. Remove from heat, let cool for 5 minutes. Place half of the mixture in a blender; blend for 30 seconds. Pour back into stockpot and keep warm. Over low heat, melt butter, whisk in flour, one tablespoon at a time. Pour in half-and-half all at once. Continue to whisk over low heat until thick and boiling. Return asparagus mixture to medium heat and slowly add flour mixture, whisking constantly. Continue whisking until mixture begins to boil. Add salt and pepper to taste. Makes 4 servings.

Fill your home with love at Christmastime...bake cookies, sing carols and snuggle around the fire.

Carabaccia

The Governor's Inn
Ludlow, VT

A visit to Italy inspired this delicious soup recipe.

6 red onions, finely sliced
6 T. olive oil
6 c. beef broth
6 c. chicken broth
1 c. almonds, finely ground

1 t. cinnamon
1 t. nutmeg
salt and pepper to taste
Garnish: amaretto cookies,
    crumbled

Sauté onions in olive oil until transparent. Stir in beef and chicken broths and almonds; simmer for one hour. Purée mixture in a blender, a little at a time, then return to stockpot. Add cinnamon, nutmeg, salt and pepper and bring to a boil. Spoon soup into individual serving bowls, sprinkle with cookie crumbs. Makes 12 servings.

Serve dinner with light-hearted holiday fun...woolly mittens will hold silverware and napkins while brightly checked mufflers stand in as place mats.

154

Festive Feasting

Country Beef Stew

Debbie Johnston
Cottage Grove, OR

A thick, hearty soup that's perfect for serving in bread bowls.

1/2 lb. bacon, chopped
2 lbs. stew meat, cubed
1 c. onion, diced
3 to 4 stalks celery, chopped
14-1/2 oz. can tomatoes,
   chopped
3 cloves garlic, minced
1/2 t. dried sage

1/2 t. dried thyme
1/2 t. dried marjoram
2 c. beef broth
salt and pepper to taste
4 to 5 potatoes, peeled and
   quartered
4 to 5 carrots, sliced

Fry bacon in a large Dutch oven until brown. Add stew meat, brown over high heat. Reduce heat to medium-low and stir in onion, celery, tomatoes, garlic, sage, thyme and marjoram. Blend in beef broth, salt and pepper. Cover and simmer for 2 hours. Add potatoes and carrots. Cook an additional 30 to 40 minutes. Makes 6 to 8 servings.

Sausage-Potato Chowder

Carol Wakefield
Indianapolis, IN

We start making this soup when the first hint of frost's in the air.

1 lb. smoked sausage, chopped
2 T. butter
1 onion, chopped
1/2 c. celery, sliced
3 c. potatoes, cubed

3 c. chicken broth
1/2 c. sour cream
10-3/4 oz. cream of mushroom
   soup
1 c. milk

Melt butter in Dutch oven and sauté onions and celery until onion become translucent. Add potatoes and chicken broth; bring to a boil. Cover, reduce heat and simmer until potatoes are tender, about 15 to 20 minutes. In small bowl, combine sour cream and mushroom soup, add to chowder, then stir in milk. Heat, but do not boil. Makes 6 to 8 servings.

The very name of Christmas,
All that's merry,
sweet and gay,
and may it bring
the very thing
you long for most
this happy day.

–Antique postcard

Festive Feasting

Tomato-Rice Soup

Lynn Menapace
Gallup, NM

While my children were growing up, we always enjoyed a bowl of this warming soup on cold, snowy evenings. It's simple to make, and it seems the ingredients are always on hand.

1 c. onion, chopped
1/2 c. celery, chopped
1 T. butter
1 lb. ground beef
28-oz. can diced tomatoes,
    undrained

2 cubes beef bouillon
1/3 c. rice, uncooked
1 t. salt
1/2 t. chili powder
2-1/2 c. water

Combine onion, celery and butter in a stockpot, stir in beef and continue to cook until beef is well browned; drain. Add tomatoes, bouillon, rice, salt, chili powder and water. Bring to a boil, then reduce heat and simmer, covered, for 30 minutes. Makes 4 servings.

Make your own snow globe, it's easy. Use waterproof adhesive to glue a figure inside a clean, dry baby food jar lid. Fill the jar with distilled water and sprinkle in glitter. Add more waterproof adhesive to the inside of the jar lid; tighten down and let dry.

Warm Red-Skinned Potato Salad

Mary Schlagel
Warwick, NY

Warm or even served cold the next day, you'll love this!

3 to 4 lbs. red-skinned potatoes,
  boiled and coarsely chopped
3 stalks celery, chopped
1 onion, chopped
1 green pepper, chopped
1/2 red pepper, chopped
1 carrot, sliced
2 c. mayonnaise
1/2 c. sour cream
3 T. Dijon mustard

2 to 3 sprigs fresh parsley,
  snipped
1 t. salt
1/2 t. pepper
1/8 t. paprika
1 t. sugar
1 t. vinegar
Garnish: carrot curls and fresh
  parsley sprigs

Toss together potatoes, celery, onion, peppers and carrot. In a separate bowl, blend mayonnaise, sour cream, Dijon mustard, parsley, salt, pepper, paprika, sugar and vinegar; whisk until smooth. Pour over top of warm potatoes and gently mix until coated; serve warm. Garnish with carrot curls and fresh parsley sprigs. Makes 6 to 8 servings.

What are your favorite things to do during Christmas?
"Baking cookies, pies and decorating the Christmas tree."

Kelli, age 6

Festive Feasting

Cashew Salad

Kate Saunier
Grand Rapids, MI

A wonderfully crunchy salad!

1 head lettuce, torn
8-oz. pkg. shredded Swiss
    cheese
1 c. oil
3/4 c. sugar
1/3 c. vinegar
salt to taste

1 t. mustard
1 t. onion, grated
1 T. poppy seed
1 c. cashews
1 c. croutons
Garnish: croutons

Toss together lettuce and Swiss cheese in a medium serving bowl. In a separate bowl, whisk together oil, sugar, vinegar, salt, mustard, onion and poppy seed. Before serving, add cashews, croutons and dressing to lettuce and cheese; toss to coat. Garnish with croutons. Makes 6 to 8 servings.

Celebration Cranberry Salad

Linda Zell
Delavan, WI

We especially love this served with ham or pork roast.

8-oz. can crushed pineapple,
    drained and juice reserved
16-oz. can whole berry
    cranberry sauce

6-oz. pkg. raspberry gelatin
1-1/2 c. boiling water

Pour reserved pineapple juice in a 2-cup measuring cup, then add enough cold water to equal 1-1/2 cups liquid. Combine cranberry sauce and pineapple; set side. Dissolve gelatin in boiling water; add cranberry sauce mixture and reserved juice. Combine thoroughly and pour into an 8"x8" glass dish; chill 4 to 6 hours, then cut into squares to serve. Makes 9 servings.

Crunchy Cole Slaw

Darleen Miller
Centerville, GA

*I took this salad to a potluck and the club president got so many
requests for the recipe, it was published in the club newsletter!*

1 c. oil
1/2 c. sugar
1/3 c. vinegar
2 3-oz. pkgs. beef ramen
   noodles with seasoning
   packets, divided

1 c. slivered almonds
1 bunch green onions, finely
   chopped
16-oz. pkg. cole slaw
1 c. roasted sunflower seeds

Whisk together oil, sugar, vinegar and seasoning packets; set aside.
Break ramen noodles into small pieces and toss with slivered almonds.
Spread in a single layer on an ungreased baking sheet and toast at
350 degrees for 5 to 8 minutes. Combine coleslaw and onions, stir in
noodle mixture, sunflower seeds and dressing; toss to coat. Serve
immediately. Makes 10 to 12 servings.

Christmas...is not an eternal event at all, but a piece of
one's home that one carries in one's heart.

-Freya Stark

Festive Feasting

Great Greek Salad

Kathryn DeLeurere
Hobart, IN

Adds just the finishing touch to any great pasta dish.

10 c. mixed greens, torn
1 cucumber, sliced
1 red onion, thinly sliced
1 tomato, chopped
3-1/4 oz. can black olives,
   drained
8 oz. feta cheese, crumbled
1 c. croutons

1/4 c. olive oil
1/4 c. lemon juice
2 cloves garlic, crushed
1 pkt. granulated sugar
   substitute
pepper to taste
dried oregano, marjoram and
   thyme to taste

Blend mixed greens, cucumber, onion, tomato, olives, feta cheese and croutons. Combine olive oil, lemon juice, garlic, sugar substitute and seasonings in a jar with a tight fitting lid; shake well. Pour dressing over salad before serving; toss to coat. Makes 6 to 8 servings.

Do you have a pocketful of Christmas wishes? Stencil "wishes" on a piece of flannel, then blanket stitch to a pillow...tuck your wishes inside.

Cinnamon-Applesauce Salad

Hilary Ryder
Boonville, NY

The combination of these different ingredients results in a truly delicious salad...you'll be pleasantly surprised.

1/3 c. red cinnamon candies
1 c. boiling water
3-oz. pkg. lemon gelatin
1 c. applesauce
8-oz. pkg. cream cheese,
    softened

1/2 c. mayonnaise
1/2 c. celery, chopped
1/2 c. chopped walnuts

Add cinnamon candies to boiling water; stir to dissolve. Pour candy mixture over lemon gelatin stir to blend, then add applesauce. Spoon applesauce mixture in an 8"x8" pan; chill until firm. Combine remaining ingredients and spread over gelatin; chill again for 2 to 4 hours, or until firm. Makes 6 to 8 servings.

Nothing's better on a snow day than building a snowman!
Keep a box filled with everything the kids will
need...mittens, scarf, hat and buttons. Don't forget a
camera too, there's sure to be lots of fun.

Festive Feasting

Layered Apricot Salad

Kathy McEntyre
Stinnett, TX

Layer this in a clear trifle dish for a really beautiful presentation.

20-oz. can crushed pineapple, juice reserved
15-1/4 oz. can apricots, chopped and juice reserved

6-oz. pkg. orange gelatin
2 c. boiling water
1/2 c. mini marshmallows
1/2 c. chopped pecans

Drain fruit and keep juices in separate bowls. Dissolve orange gelatin in boiling water. Measure one cup reserved pineapple juice and one cup apricot juice; add to gelatin mixture. Stir in pineapple and apricots. Pour into a 2-quart serving dish and cover with marshmallows and pecans. Chill until firm.

Topping:

1 c. pineapple juice
1 c. apricot juice
1 egg, beaten
1/2 c. sugar

2 T. all-purpose flour
2 T. shortening
1/2 pt. whipping cream

Combine juices, egg, sugar and flour. Cook over medium heat until mixture thickens; stir constantly. Add shortening, stir to blend and refrigerate until cool. Fold in whipped cream and spread over chilled gelatin. Makes 10 servings.

Sort through Grandma's button box and string the prettiest ones on heavy elastic...a nostalgic bracelet.

Christmas Salad

Pam Hoerner
Davenport, IA

Just a hint of cranberry makes this salad a nice refreshing addition to any holiday dinner.

1 c. cranberries, ground
3/4 c. sugar
8-oz. pkg. cream cheese,
  softened

1 c. mini marshmallows
1/2 c. chopped walnuts
1 banana, sliced
8 oz. whipped topping

Mix cranberries and sugar. Cover and let stand overnight in the refrigerator. The next day, beat cream cheese with mixer until light and fluffy. Add cranberry mixture and stir only until blended. Add remaining ingredients except whipped topping. When thoroughly mixed, fold in whipped topping. Makes 10 to 12 servings.

Thread a vintage button on wire, then attach to the center of your bow...what a pretty package topper.

Festive Feasting

Riviera Salad

Mary Schmidt
Bangor, WI

A colorful salad...so pretty on a holiday buffet table.

1/4 c. whole pecans
1 T. plus 1 t. sugar
1/2 head Romaine lettuce, torn
1/2 head iceburg lettuce, torn
1/4 c. red onion, thinly sliced

1 c. strawberries, sliced
1/2 c. mayonnaise
1/4 c. half-and-half
1 c. sugar
1 to 2 T. poppy seeds

Combine pecans and sugar in a skillet over medium heat, stirring constantly, until sugar melts and the nuts are golden. Spread mixture on wax paper to cool; set aside. Toss together Romaine and iceburg lettuce; add onion, strawberries and nuts. Whisk remaining ingredients and pour over salad. Makes 6 to 8 servings.

Delicious Pea Salad

Jane McLaughlin
Lighthouse Point, FL

Cashews and bacon together; it really is delicious!

10-oz. pkg. frozen peas, thawed
1 c. cauliflower, chopped
1/4 c. green onion, diced
1 c. chopped cashews

1/2 c. sour cream
1 c. ranch salad dressing
6 slices bacon, crisply cooked
   and crumbled

Combine all ingredients in a large bowl. Chill overnight or at least 4 hours so flavors can blend. Makes 6 servings.

Fresh from the oven croutons are easy to make and delicious tossed in soups or salads...give a jarful as a hostess gift.

Butternut Squash Soufflé

Elizabeth Elliott
Ripon, CA

Slightly sweet and gingery.

2 c. butternut squash, cooked
1/4 c. butter
3/4 c. sugar
3 eggs, beaten

1 c. milk
1/2 t. ground ginger
1/2 t. coconut flavoring
1/2 c. flaked coconut

Combine first 7 ingredients together in an ungreased 2-quart baking dish. Bake, uncovered, at 350 degrees for 15 minutes; sprinkle coconut over top. Bake an additional 15 minutes or until set. Serves 6 to 8.

Cranberry Applesauce

Robbin Chamberlain
Worthington, OH

So festive and colorful when spooned in a glass serving dish.

3/4 lb. cranberries
1-1/2 c. water
3/4 c. sugar

4 lbs. apples, cored and
    quartered
Garnish: cinnamon

Place cranberries, water, sugar and apples in a large saucepan. Cover and simmer for 20 minutes or until apples are soft. Cool slightly and press mixture through a sieve or food mill. Sprinkle with cinnamon before serving. Makes about 8 cups.

Festive Feasting

Pommes Anna

Deborah Wells
Broken Arrow, OK

You'll love these crispy potatoes...they're heavenly!

4 to 5 potatoes, sliced
1 t. salt
1/2 t. pepper
1/4 c. butter, melted

2 cloves garlic, pressed
2 onions, thinly sliced
9 T. grated Parmesan cheese,
   divided

Place potatoes in a large mixing bowl, cover with ice water and let stand for 15 minutes. Drain and dry potatoes, then sprinkle with salt and pepper. Combine butter and garlic; place in a 2-1/2 quart ungreased baking dish and heat at 425 degrees until butter sizzles. Remove from oven and skim off the white foam. Arrange 1/3 of potatoes and onions in an overlapping pattern in the bottom of the dish; top with 1/3 of the butter mixture and 3 tablespoons Parmesan cheese. Repeat the same layering 2 more times. Bake, covered, at 400 degrees for one hour or until potatoes are tender. Uncover and place under broiler 6 inches from heat source for 4 to 5 minutes or until golden. Makes 6 servings.

What do the reindeer & elves do after Christmas is over?
"The elves ride the reindeer and they play."

Austin, age 7

Honeyed Maple Carrots

Wendy Paffenroth
Pine Island, NY

Maple, honey and cinnamon make such a tasty glaze.

2 lbs. baby carrots
2 T. butter
1/2 c. honey

2 T. maple syrup
1/8 t. cinnamon

Place carrots in a large saucepan, cover with water and boil until fork tender. Drain and place in an ungreased 1-1/2 quart baking dish or deep dish pie plate. Melt butter in a saucepan; stir in honey and maple syrup. Pour mixture over carrots and stir to coat; sprinkle with cinnamon. Bake, uncovered, at 325 degrees for 10 to 15 minutes. Makes 4 to 6 servings.

Green Beans Supreme

SueMary Burford-Smith
Tulsa, OK

This isn't your usual green bean casserole. Loaded with cheese and sour cream, it will be your new favorite!

1 onion, sliced
1 T. fresh parsley, snipped
3 T. butter, divided
2 T. all-purpose flour
1/2 t. lemon zest
1/2 t. salt
1/8 t. pepper

1/2 c. milk
1 c. sour cream
2 9-oz. pkgs. frozen
   French-style green
   beans, cooked
1/2 c. shredded Cheddar cheese
1/4 c. bread crumbs

Cook onion and parsley in 2 tablespoons butter until onion is tender. Blend in flour, lemon zest, salt and pepper. Stir milk; heat until thick and bubbly. Add sour cream and beans; heat through. Spoon into an ungreased 2-quart baking dish; sprinkle with cheese. Melt remaining butter and toss with bread crumbs; sprinkle on top of beans. Broil 3 to 4 inches from heat source until golden. Makes 4 to 6 servings.

168

Festive Feasting

Holiday Yams

Jamie Ruggerio
Orcutt, CA

It's just not the holiday season without these yams.

1/2 c. all-purpose flour
1/2 c. brown sugar, packed
1/2 c. quick-cooking oats,
   uncooked
1 t. cinnamon

1/3 c. butter, melted
2 17-oz. cans yams, drained
1 c. cranberries
1-1/2 c. mini marshmallows

Combine flour, sugar, oats, cinnamon and butter until mixture resembles coarse crumbs. Measure out one cup, reserving the remainder. In a separate mixing bowl, stir together one cup crumb mixture with drained yams and cranberries. Place in a greased 8"x8" baking dish. Top with remaining crumb mixture. Bake, uncovered, at 350 degrees for 35 minutes. Layer marshmallows on top and place under broiler 4 to 5 inches from heat source for 2 to 3 minutes or until golden. Makes 6 to 8 servings.

Many merry Christmases, friendships,
great accumulation of cheerful recollections,
affection on earth...heaven at last for all of us.

-Charles Dickens

Baked Stuffed Tomatoes

Donna Dye
London, OH

Rediscover this old-fashioned favorite...it's as good as ever!

2 tomatoes
1/4 c. dry bread crumbs
2 t. butter, melted
1/2 t. grated Parmesan cheese

1/4 t. dried basil
1/4 t. dried oregano
1 t. fresh parsley, finely chopped
salt and pepper to taste

Slice tomatoes in half; set aside. Blend together bread crumbs, butter, cheese, basil, oregano, parsley, salt and pepper. Spoon crumb mixture on each tomato half; pressing firmly. Place tomato halves in a greased 9" baking dish and bake at 350 degrees for 20 minutes or until topping is golden. Makes 4 servings.

Snowflake stockings are so simple to make. Sew a variety of buttons in different sizes and colors to your stocking, then just add a straight stitch to turn them into snowflakes.

Festive Feasting

Cornbread Dressing

Helen Murray
Piketon, OH

A snap to prepare and it's a really tasty change from the more traditional bread stuffing.

4 c. cornbread, cubed
2 c. bread, cubed
1/2 c. green pepper, chopped
1 c. onion, chopped
1/2 c. celery, chopped

2 10-oz. cans chicken broth
2 eggs, beaten
2 T. dried sage
salt and pepper to taste

Lay cornbread and bread on parchment paper overnight to dry. When ready to prepare dressing, gently toss cornbread and bread cubes with green pepper, onion, celery, chicken broth, eggs, sage, salt and pepper; blending well. Spoon in a greased 9"x9" baking dish and bake at 350 degrees for 45 minutes. Makes 6 servings.

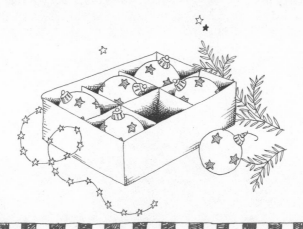

When Santa & Mrs. Claus take a vacation, where do they go?
"I think they go to Florida and go to Disney World. Santa wears a t-shirt and shorts because it's so hot there. But people still know it's Santa."

Elizabeth, age 7

Pasta Con Broccoli

Anne Messier
Sacramento, CA

I remember both Mom & Dad in the kitchen preparing holiday meals...Mom roasting the turkey and Dad making this recipe. Finally, when dinner was ready, we'd all gather around an old oak table to enjoy it together.

1/2 c. onion, chopped
1 T. butter
2 T. oil
5-oz. can tomato sauce
1 c. water
Italian seasoning
salt to taste
1/8 t. pepper

1 lb. rigatoni, cooked and drained
1 lb. broccoli, cooked and drained
1-1/2 c. bread crumbs, buttered and browned
1/2 c. grated Parmesan cheese

Sauté onion in butter and oil. Add tomato sauce, water, seasoning, salt and pepper. Simmer for 20 to 30 minutes. On platter or large serving dish, place cooked rigatoni, top with broccoli, tomato sauce mixture, bread crumbs and Parmesan cheese. Serves 4 to 6.

A bowl of lady apples and pomanders makes a pretty centerpiece...tuck in some greenery sprigs or holly.

Festive Feasting

Asparagus Pie

Brenda Colvin
Wheeling, WV

At our family dinners, this is almost more important than the turkey!

3 10-oz. cans asparagus,
  drained
1-1/2 c. shredded Cheddar
  cheese

1 c. mayonnaise
1/2 c. green onion, chopped
3 egg whites

Place asparagus in an ungreased 9" pie plate. Combine cheese, mayonnaise and onion in a separate bowl. Beat egg whites until stiff, but not dry; fold into cheese mixture. Spread over asparagus and bake, uncovered, 20 minutes at 350 degrees. Makes 6 servings.

Let guests help themselves to bottles of juice and
water chilling in festive red or green
enamelware pails.

Cranberry-Orange Bread

Jennifer Niemi
Nova Scotia, Canada

Every fall my mum and I help organize a bake sale for our local animal shelter. One year I arrived with these loaves still warm from the oven; the sweet aroma filling the air. Before I knew it people flocked to the table and the bread was gone in a matter of minutes!

2 c. all-purpose flour
2 t. baking powder
1/2 t. baking soda
1/4 t. salt
2 t. ground cloves
1 c. sugar

1 c. orange juice
1 egg, beaten
1/2 c. margarine, melted
1 c. cranberries, halved
zest of one orange

Sift together flour, baking powder, baking soda, salt, cloves and sugar; set aside. Blend together orange juice, egg and margarine. Make a well in the center of the dry ingredients and add the orange juice mixture to the center. Stir until the flour is moistened, then fold in cranberries and orange zest. Pour into a greased 9"x5" loaf pan. Bake at 350 degrees for 45 minutes, or until a knife inserted in the center comes out clean. Makes 6 to 8 servings.

Pillar candles set in a minnow bucket
give off a magical glow.

Festive Feasting

One Bowl Banana Bread

Diana Yeager
Columbus, Ohio

*I've also used canned pineapple, draining half the juice, or fresh
apples in this recipe...just as moist and wonderful!*

1/3 c. oil
3 bananas, mashed
1/2 t. vanilla extract
3 eggs

2-1/3 c. biscuit baking mix
1 c. sugar
1/2 c. chopped walnuts

Beat together all ingredients for about 30 seconds. Pour batter into a
greased 9"x5" loaf pan. Bake at 350 degrees for 35 to 45 minutes or
until toothpick inserted in center comes out clean. Makes 6 to
8 servings.

Hang mittens or stockings on the backs of chairs and fill
with goodies...clever party favors!

Apple-Walnut Bread

Barbara Wise
Jamestown, OH

Moist and sweet, with yummy apples and walnuts throughout.

3 eggs
2 c. sugar
1-1/4 c. oil
1 t. salt
1/2 t. cinnamon

2 t. vanilla extract
3 c. all-purpose flour
1-1/2 t. baking soda
3 c. apples, finely chopped
1 c. chopped walnuts

Beat eggs with sugar; add oil, salt, cinnamon and vanilla. Stir in flour, baking soda, apples and nuts; dough will be very thick. Place in 2, greased 9"x5" loaf pans and bake at 325 degrees for one hour or until center tests done. Makes about 12 to 16 servings.

What kind of snacks do reindeer like?
"They only eat carrots, lettuce and cabbage."

Brooke, age 8

Festive Feasting

Orange Biscuits

Peg Baker
La Rue, OH

My grandmother kept a journal and always included lots of recipes alongside her memories. I remember her always serving these with ham and oh, the aroma from the kitchen was wonderful.

1/2 c. orange juice
3/4 c. sugar, divided
1/4 c. butter
2 t. orange zest
2 c. all-purpose flour
1 T. baking powder

1/2 t. salt
1/4 c. shortening
3/4 c. milk
1/2 c. butter, melted
1/2 t. cinnamon

Combine orange juice, 1/2 cup sugar, butter and orange zest in a medium saucepan. Cook and stir over medium heat for 2 minutes. Fill 12 ungreased muffin tins about 2/3 full; set aside. Sift together flour, baking powder and salt; cut in shortening until mixture resembles coarse crumbs. Stir in milk and mix with a fork until mixture forms a ball. On a lightly floured surface, knead dough for one minute. Roll into a 9-inch square about 1/2-inch thick; brush with melted butter. Combine cinnamon and remaining sugar; sprinkle over butter. Roll up and cut into 12 slices about 3/4-inch thick. Place slices cut side down over orange mixture in muffin cups. Bake at 450 degrees for 12 to 15 minutes. Cool for 2 to 3 minutes; remove from pan. Makes 12 biscuits.

Cheddar-Basil Biscuits

Matt DeVolder
Ellsworth, KS

Simple to make, you can have warm biscuits for dinner anytime!

2 c. biscuit baking mix
1/2 c. shredded Cheddar cheese
2/3 c. milk

1/2 t. dried basil
1/2 t. garlic powder
1/4 c. butter, melted

Stir together biscuit mix, cheese and milk until a soft dough forms,
then beat vigorously for 30 seconds. Drop by heaping tablespoonfuls
onto an ungreased baking sheet. Bake at 450 degrees for 10 to
12 minutes or until golden. Combine basil, garlic powder and butter;
brush over hot biscuits. Makes 10 to 12 biscuits.

Everyone's bound to come in with wet mittens, scarves
and hats after a day of snowy fun...why not make a
snowman peg rack to hang by the back door? So
clever...wood painted with cheery faces and
orange dowels for pegs.

Festive Feasting

Feather Rolls

Jo Ann

Just like the name...light as a feather.

1 pkg. dry active yeast	3/4 t. salt
1/4 c. warm water	1 egg
4 T. butter, softened	3/4 c. warm milk
1 T. sugar	2 c. all-purpose flour

Dissolve yeast in water; let stand 5 minutes to dissolve. Blend together butter, sugar, salt, egg and milk; add to yeast mixture. Beat until smooth, add flour and beat until well blended. Cover and set in a warm place for one hour or until double in size. Punch down dough and divide in 12 portions; roll each in a ball. Place in greased muffin tins, cover and let rise for 30 minutes. Bake at 400 degrees for 15 to 20 minutes or until golden brown. Makes 12 servings.

Think "magic" as you set your dinner table. Use lots of white votives and sparkly glass serving bowls. Pull out Grandma's dishes, too...a blend of old and new that will bring sweet memories.

Chocolate Chip-Pumpkin Bread

Susan Sherman
Ashville, OH

A moist bread that freezes well...make several for holiday gifts!

3 c. sugar
15-oz. can pumpkin
1 c. oil
2/3 c. water
4 eggs
3-1/2 c. all-purpose flour
1 T. cinnamon

1 T. nutmeg
2 T. baking soda
1-1/2 t. salt
1 c. mini semi-sweet chocolate
   chips
1/2 c. chopped walnuts

Blend together sugar, pumpkin, oil, water and eggs; beat until smooth.
Add flour, cinnamon, nutmeg, baking soda and salt; stir in chocolate
chips and walnuts. Divide equally among 3 greased and floured
9"x5" loaf pans. Bake at 350 degrees for one hour or until a knife
inserted in the center comes out clean. Cool on wire racks before
removing from pans. Makes 3 loaves.

Hang extra mirrors during the holidays and light lots of
candles for a magical holiday glow.

Festive Feasting

Raisin-Rosemary Bread

Kathy Unruh
Fesno, CA

This never lasts long...better make some extras and freeze for later!

3 c. golden raisins
3 c. milk, scalded
2 c. sugar
6 T. butter, softened
3 eggs
1 t. vanilla extract

4-1/2 c. all-purpose flour
2 t. salt
2 T. baking powder
2 T. fresh rosemary, crushed or
   2 teaspoons dried rosemary
2 c. walnuts, coarsely chopped

Stir raisins in milk, cover and cool for 30 minutes or until lukewarm. Beat sugar and butter, add cooled raisin mixture, eggs and vanilla; mix well. Whisk together flour, salt, baking powder, rosemary and nuts until well combined; add to raisin mixture. Divide equally among 2 greased and floured 9"x5" loaf pans. Bake at 350 degrees for 35 to 40 minutes or until golden and center tests done. Cool 10 minutes, then remove from pans and place on racks to cool completely. Makes 2 loaves.

Look for ice cube trays in clever shapes...stars can be filled with cranberry juice and added to the punch bowl.

Cider-Baked Ham

Kelly Hall
Butler, MO

On Christmas Eve I baked this ham and took it, along with all the trimmings, to Grandpa's house for a surprise dinner. We had a lovely day together and a white Christmas, too!

12 to 14-lb. cooked ham
2 c. apple cider
1 stick cinnamon
1 t. whole cloves

1/2 t. allspice
1/2 c. brown sugar, packed
1/2 c. honey
Garnish: whole cloves

Place ham in a shallow, roasting pan. Combine apple cider, cinnamon, cloves and allspice in a small saucepan; heat to boiling. Cover and simmer for 5 minutes; pour over ham. Bake, uncovered, at 325 degrees, basting every 30 minutes with cider sauce for about 3 hours. Remove ham from oven. Increase oven temperature to 400 degrees. Score diagonal lines in fat with the tip of a knife to form diamond shapes, being careful not to cut into meat. Stud each diamond with a whole clove. Combine brown sugar and honey in a small saucepan. Cook over low heat, stirring until sugar is melted. Brush over top of ham. Return ham to 400 degree oven. Bake 30 additional minutes, brushing the ham every 10 minutes with remaining honey mixture until brown and glistening and meat thermometer registers 160 degrees. Remove from oven. Let stand 20 minutes before slicing. Makes 24 to 26 servings.

Festive Feasting

Friendship Quiche

Susan Kennedy
Gooseberry Patch

*Invite friends over for a holiday get-together and serve this simple
to make quiche. Add a crisp salad and some rolls, then settle in
around the table and catch up on each other's holiday plans.*

1/2 c. sliced mushrooms
1/2 c. broccoli, chopped
1/2 c. cooked, ham, diced
2 T. butter
9-inch pie crust, baked
8-oz. pkg. Cheddar cheese,
   cubed

1-1/2 c. milk
3 eggs
salt to taste
nutmeg to taste
pepper to taste

Sauté vegetables and ham in butter, spoon in crust and top with
cheese. Combine milk, eggs and spices in blender and pour over
cheese and vegetables. Bake, uncovered, at 450 degrees for
15 minutes. Reduce heat to 350 degrees and bake an additional
10 to 15 minutes. Let sit for 5 minutes before cutting. Makes 6 to
8 servings.

What's your favorite treat to leave Santa and why?
"Cookies because he likes the sprinkles."
Zachary, age 5

Honey-Glazed Turkey Breast

Adrienne Payne
Omaha, NE

Just the right size for a family dinner.

1/4 c. honey
1 T. Dijon mustard
1 T. Worcestershire sauce
1 T. margarine, melted

1-3/4 to 2-lb. turkey breast
1 T. oil
1/4 t. salt
1/8 t. pepper

Stir together honey, mustard, Worcestershire and margarine; set aside. Rinse turkey breast and pat dry. Place in a shallow roasting pan, brush with oil, then sprinkle with salt and pepper. Insert a meat thermometer into the thickest part of the breast, being sure not to touch the bone. Roast turkey, uncovered, at 325 degrees for 1-1/4 to 1-1/2 hours or until juices run clear and the thermometer registers 170 degrees. Brush turkey breast with honey glaze several times during the last 15 minutes. Transfer turkey to cutting board; let stand for 10 to 15 minutes before carving. Heat remaining glaze and serve with turkey. Makes 6 servings.

Reindeer Treats

When Santa & Mrs. Claus take a vacation, where do they go?
"Washington, Oregon or Nevada to see all the cool stuff."

Jason, age 7

Festive Feasting

Spinach Lasagna

Michelle Campen
Peoria, IL

Shared with us by a foreign exchange student from China, this lasagna is really delicious and a nice change from the more traditional meat and cheese lasagna.

1 lb. ground beef
1/2 c. onion, chopped
1 clove garlic, minced
1 T. oil
8-oz. can tomato sauce
8-oz. can tomato paste
1/2 c. water
1 t. salt

1/2 t. oregano
2 eggs, beaten
10-oz. pkg. frozen, chopped
    spinach, thawed
8-oz. carton cottage cheese
12-oz. pkg. lasagna, cooked
8 slices American cheese

Cook ground beef, onion and garlic in oil until meat is browned. Stir in tomato sauce, tomato paste, water, salt and oregano; mix well and simmer for 15 minutes. Combine eggs, spinach and cottage cheese; mix well. Layer ingredients in an ungreased 13"x9" baking dish as follows: a small amount of sauce in the bottom of dish, noodles, filling and additional noodles, spoon sauce over all. Repeat layers, ending with sauce. Cover with aluminum foil and bake at 350 degrees for 45 minutes. Remove aluminum foil and arrange cheese slices over casserole. Bake, uncovered, an additional 15 minutes. Cut into squares and serve. Makes 6 to 8 servings.

Chicken Cordon Bleu

Shaunie Marshall
Salt Lake City, UT

An elegant holiday dinner you can make in your slow cooker.

2 eggs
2 c. milk, divided
1 T. dried, minced onion
8 slices bread, cubed and crusts
   removed
12 thin slices cooked ham, rolled
   up

8-oz. pkg. shredded Swiss
   cheese
2-1/2 c. chicken, cooked and ,
   cubed
10-3/4 oz. can cream of chicken
   soup

Beat eggs and 1-1/2 cups milk together; stir in onion and bread cubes.
Place half of the mixture in a 3-1/2 quart slow cooker; top with half of
the rolled up ham, cheese and chicken. Combine soup and remaining
milk and pour half over chicken. Repeat layers again, topping with
remaining soup mixture. Cover and cook on low for 4 to 5 hours or
until a thermometer inserted in the bread mixture reads 160 degrees.
Makes 8 to 10 servings.

Children's toys are always a warm-hearted and
sentimental way to decorate for the holidays. Piled in
a wagon, sitting under a tree or arranged on a mantel,
they're sure to bring back special memories.

Festive Feasting

Maple Roast Chicken & Veggies
Jo Ann

A tender, juicy chicken with sweet vegetables.

1 winter squash, peeled and
    chopped
3 to 4 parsnips, peeled and
    chopped
2 stalks celery, chopped
2 carrots, chopped
1 onion, chopped

1 sweet potato, chopped
6 to 7-lb. chicken
2 T. butter, melted
1/2 t. salt
1/4 t. pepper
1/2 t. dried rosemary
1/2 c. maple syrup

Spread vegetables evenly in a lightly oiled roasting pan; place chicken
on top. Brush chicken with butter; sprinkle with salt, pepper and
rosemary. Place on lowest rack in oven and bake at 400 degrees for
1-1/2 to 2 hours or until juices run clear. Baste about every 10 minutes
with maple syrup and pan juices. Remove from oven and let stand
10 minutes before carving. Makes 4 to 6 servings.

Fragrant paperwhites tucked in red speckled pots look
pretty on a mantel or windowsill.

Hearty Chicken Pie

Colleen Vasconcellos
Miami, FL

You can use any combination of vegetables and even substitute cooked turkey if you'd like...so warm and filling.

2 9-inch refrigerated pie crusts, unbaked
2 c. chicken, cooked
15-oz. can mixed vegetables
8-oz. can corn, drained
1 t. dried parsley

1 t. dried basil
2 c. milk
4 T. all-purpose flour
salt and pepper to taste
1 egg, beaten

Place one pie crust in a lightly oiled 9" pie pan; top with chicken and vegetables; stir. Bring remaining ingredients to a boil in a small saucepan; stirring constantly. Reduce heat to medium and continue to stir until mixture thickens. Pour over chicken and vegetables, then cover with second pie crust. Crimp edges to seal crusts and vent top, then brush pie crust with egg. Bake at 325 degrees for 30 minutes or until golden. Makes 6 to 8 servings.

Toss orange peel and cinnamon sticks in the fireplace for a sweet fragrance!

Festive Feasting

Apricot Porkloin

Angela Nichols
Mt. Airy, NC

The apricot sauce gives this roast a sweet glaze.

4-lb. boneless porkloin, tied for
   roasting
seasoning salt to taste
15-1/4 oz. can apricot halves,
   juice reserved

1 c. sugar
1/2 c. water
1 t. lemon juice

Spray a 13"x9" glass baking dish with non-sick vegetable spray. Place
porkloin in baking dish; add seasoning salt. Bake at 325 degrees,
covered, for 2-1/2 to 3 hours, or until a meat thermometer registers
160 degrees; let rest 10 minutes. Combine apricot halves with 1/4 cup
juice; break apart apricot halves and mash. Blend in sugar, water
and lemon juice. Bring to a boil and cook 2 to 3 minutes; remove
from heat. Slice porkloin and pour apricot sauce over slices. Makes
8 servings.

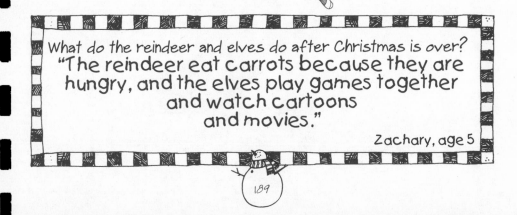

What do the reindeer and elves do after Christmas is over?
"The reindeer eat carrots because they are
hungry, and the elves play games together
and watch cartoons
and movies."

Zachary, age 5

Family & Friends

Christmas Day...make it a day of fun-filled memories!

Watch all the parades or pop your favorite holiday movie in the VCR...it's a great way to unwind after the morning's excitement. You might even sneak in a little nap!

Build a cozy fire, toast marshmallows, make s'mores...yum!

After dinner, linger at the table. Pull out all the holiday cards or letters you've received and share your favorites.

Visit friends and neighbors...it's fun to see what Santa brought them!

Encourage everyone to sing favorite Christmas carols...it doesn't matter if you're off key, you'll be sensational!

Get outside! Take a walk, build a snowman, go sledding...enjoy the day together.

Before everyone goes to bed, hold hands and say a prayer...make this a Christmas to remember always.

Snowman Kit

Sweet Treats

Always save the best for last!

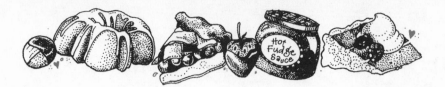

Fruit Pudding Cake

Shannon Thomas
Stillwater, PA

My husband's grandmother created this pudding cake recipe. You can use any of your favorite fruit...it's one of those tried & true recipes.

1 c. sugar
2 T. shortening
3/4 c. milk
1-1/2 c. all-purpose flour

2 t. baking powder
1 c. sugar
2 c. fruit, chopped
1-1/2 c. hot water

Combine sugar, shortening and milk; pour into a greased 8"x8" baking dish. In a separate mixing bowl, stir together flour, baking powder, sugar and fruit; pour over top of batter. Slowly pour hot water on top; don't stir. Bake at 350 degrees for one hour. Makes 6 to 8 servings.

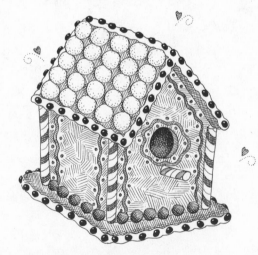

When Santa & Mrs. Claus take a vacation, where do they go?
"To the beach...play in the water, sit in the sand and get a suntan."

Conner, age 5

Sweet Treats

Grandmother's Pound Cake

Donna Foley
Omaha, NE

Very simple and old-fashioned.

1 c. margarine
1-2/3 c. sugar
5 eggs

1/2 t. vanilla extract
2 c. all-purpose flour

Beat margarine until creamy, then fold in sugar, eggs and vanilla. When thoroughly blended, add flour a little at a time. Spread batter into a greased and floured 9"x5" loaf pan. Bake at 300 degrees for one to 1-1/2 hours or until golden. Makes 8 to 10 servings.

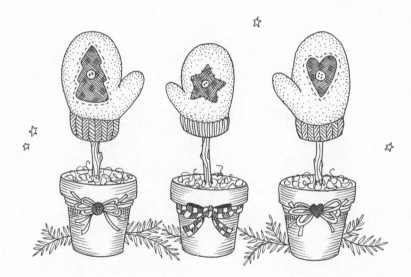

Decorate in unexpected ways...line up a trio of mitten topiaries, turn plaid winter scarves into table runners or tie bright red bows on bales of hay!

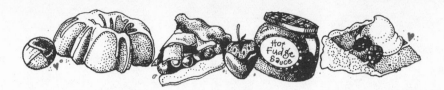

Golden Apple Crisp

Charlene Marino
Clifton Park, NY

I always get lots of compliments on this apple crisp. My son and husband like it topped with fresh whipped cream or vanilla ice cream.

1 c. biscuit baking mix
1 c. brown sugar, packed
1/4 t. cinnamon

1/4 c. butter, softened
5 c. apples, sliced

Combine first 4 ingredients; set aside. Place apples in an ungreased 9"x9" baking dish and sprinkle the cinnamon mixture on top of the apples. Bake at 375 degrees for 30 minutes or until golden. Makes 4 to 6 servings.

What kind of snacks do reindeer like?
"Regular reindeer food...the kind the teachers give us to put out."
Kelli, age 6

Sweet Treats

Chocolate-Covered Cherry Cake

Heidi Krauss
Preston, CT

A favorite candy treat in a cake!

18-1/4 oz. pkg. white cake mix
1/2 c. maraschino cherries,
    chopped and 1/4 c. juice
    reserved

12-oz. tub chocolate frosting

Prepare cake batter according to package directions, except replace 1/4 cup of water with cherry juice. Stir in chopped cherries and pour mixture into 2 greased and floured 8" cake pans. Bake at 350 degrees for 20 to 25 minutes; or 5 minutes less than indicated in directions on cake box. Let cool for 10 minutes; remove from pan and frost with chocolate frosting. Makes 16 servings.

REAL snow cones...fruit juice drizzled over freshly fallen snow!

Cranberry Delight

Rebecca Cook
San Antonio, TX

Both sweet and tart...with a crunchy golden top.

3 c. apples, chopped
2 c. cranberries
1-1/4 c. sugar
1-1/2 c. quick-cooking oats,
   uncooked

1/2 c. brown sugar, packed
1/3 c. all-purpose flour
3/4 t. salt
1/2 c. butter, melted
1/3 c. chopped walnuts

Toss apples and cranberries together; sprinkle with sugar and stir well. Place mixture into an 8"x8" baking dish coated with non-stick vegetable spray. In a separate bowl, combine oats, brown sugar, flour and salt; add butter and stir. Pour over cranberry mixture and sprinkle with walnuts. Bake, uncovered, at 350 degrees for one hour. Makes 6 to 8 servings.

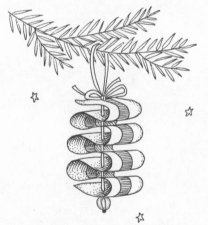

How fun...a ribbon candy ornament! Glue together colorful strips of construction paper, then slip a length of embroidery floss on a needle. Tie a knot on the bottom of the floss so it stays in place and thread through the construction paper; top with a bow.

Sweet Treats

Hot Fudge Pudding Cake

Phyliss Dixon
Fairbanks, AK

One of my favorite "comfort" foods from childhood.

1 c. buttermilk biscuit baking
   mix
1 c. sugar, divided
1/3 c. plus 3 T. baking cocoa,
   divided

1/2 c. milk
1 t. vanilla extract
1-2/3 c. hot water
Garnish: whipped topping

Stir together biscuit baking mix, 1/2 cup sugar and 3 tablespoons cocoa; blend in milk and vanilla. Spread mixture into an ungreased 8"x8" baking dish. In a separate mixing bowl, blend together remaining cocoa and sugar; sprinkle over cake mix. Pour hot water over top; do not stir. Bake at 350 degrees for 40 minutes or until top is firm to the touch. Cool slightly and serve with whipped topping. Makes 6 to 8 servings.

How do Santa & Mrs. Claus decorate their home?
"They go to the same stores at the North Pole that we do. They buy holly and talking Santas and put them up all over."

Nikki, age 5

Applesauce Brownie Cake

Suzanna Earwicker
Poway, CA

Chocolatey with crunchy almonds and a hint of cinnamon...a different brownie recipe, but so yummy! As a kid I remember sneaking bits of the sweet topping before Mom could sprinkle it on...now my kids do the same thing!

1-1/2 c. plus 2 T. sugar, divided
1/2 c. oil
2 eggs
2 c. applesauce
2 c. all-purpose flour
1-1/2 t. baking soda

1/2 t. salt
2 T. baking cocoa
1/2 t. cinnamon
1/2 c. sliced almonds
6-oz. pkg. chocolate chips

Combine 1-1/2 cups sugar, oil, eggs, applesauce, flour, baking soda, salt, cocoa and cinnamon; beat well. Pour into a greased and floured 13"x9" baking dish. Sprinkle almonds, chocolate chips and remaining sugar over all. Bake at 350 degrees for 40 to 45 minutes or until cake tester inserted in the middle comes out clean. Makes 12 to 15 servings.

What kind of snacks do reindeer like?
"They like carrots and cookies."
Kyle & Sean, ages 6 and 3

198

Sweet Treats

Nutty Cinnamon Crisps

Marsha Thomas
Huron, SD

Settle in with your favorite holiday movie and enjoy this crunchy mix.

1 c. sugar
1 c. butter
1 egg, separated
2 c. all-purpose flour

1/2 t. cinnamon
1 T. water
1/2 c. chopped nuts

Beat sugar, butter and egg yolk together; stir in flour and cinnamon. Press mixture into a lightly greased 15"x10" baking sheet. In a medium mixing bowl, beat egg white and water with fork until foamy; brush over dough. Sprinkle with nuts, then bake at 350 degrees for 20 to 25 minutes or until golden. Cut into strips and cool on wire rack. Makes 3 dozen.

Make color copies of old family photos...first birthday, school pictures, graduation and wedding days. Cut out each and glue on heavy card stock, punch a hole, then slip ribbon through...gift cards that will make everyone giggle!

Snowflake Baked Bananas

Peg Baker
La Rue, OH

The aroma of warm baked bananas and brown sugar...everyone will be back for seconds!

1/3 c. butter, melted
3 T. lemon juice
6 bananas
1/3 c. brown sugar, packed

1 t. cinnamon
1 c. flaked coconut
Garnish: maple syrup

Spread butter and lemon juice over the bottom of a lightly buttered 8"x8" baking dish; stir together until well blended. Place bananas in the dish and turn them until they are well coated. In a small mixing bowl, combine brown sugar and cinnamon; stir to blend. Sprinkle over the bananas. Bake at 375 degrees for 18 to 20 minutes. Turn bananas after the first 10 minutes of baking and sprinkle with coconut. Return to the oven for an additional 8 to 10 minutes. Serve warm with maple syrup. Makes 6 servings.

Dip the rim of a dessert glass in melted chocolate and immediately coat the chocolate with chopped nuts; refrigerate until firm. When it's time to serve dessert, add a big scoop of ice cream.

Sweet Treats

Grandma Taddie's Meringue Cake

Virginia Unger
Strongsville, OH

My wonderful mother-in-law shared this dessert with us...crispy meringue with a creamy filling, it's really sensational!

1/4 t. salt
2 t. vinegar
6 egg whites
1/2 t. vanilla extract

2 c. sugar
1 c. crushed pineapple
1/4 c. chopped nuts
1/2 pt. whipping cream, whipped

Beat salt, vinegar, egg whites and vanilla until stiff. Slowly add sugar and continue beating until very stiff. Spread on aluminum foil-lined baking sheet. Cut meringue in half with a knife, down short side of pan, before baking. Bake at 300 degrees for one to one hour and 10 minutes. Cool slightly and gently remove meringue from aluminum foil; set aside. Gently fold the pineapple and nuts into the whipping cream and spread one layer of the baked meringue with the whipped cream filling and top with the remaining layer of meringue. Cut in squares. Makes 3 dozen.

When Santa & Mrs. Claus take a vacation, where do they go?
"They come down to earth. They like to look at all of the houses to see who is good and who is bad. Then they go to a movie."

Austin, age 4

Baked Cinnamon Pudding

Rogene Rogers
Bemidji, MN

I put this in the oven to bake just as our family sits down to eat dinner. The warm scent of cinnamon is a hint that something sweet will top off the meal.

2 c. brown sugar, packed
1-1/2 c. cold water
4 T. butter, divided
1 c. sugar
1 c. milk

1-2/3 c. all-purpose flour
2 t. baking powder
2 t. cinnamon
1/2 c. chopped nuts

Blend together brown sugar, water and 2 tablespoons butter in a saucepan; bring to a boil. Combine sugar, remaining butter, milk, flour, baking powder and cinnamon; place in the bottom of an ungreased 13"x9" baking dish. Pour brown sugar mixture over top and sprinkle with nuts. Bake at 350 degrees for 45 minutes. Makes 12 servings.

How does Santa leave presents if you don't have a chimney?
"He comes through the front door and wipes his feet on the way."

Kyle & Sean, ages 6 and 3

Sweet Treats

Peppermint Stick Ice Cream Pie

Gloria Kaufmann
Orrville, OH

It isn't Christmas at our home without this pie. Make it up to a month ahead of time and freeze...what a time saver during the holidays.

2 7-oz. chocolate bars
1/2 c. margarine
4 c. crispy rice cereal

1/2 gal. peppermint stick ice cream, softened

Shave 3 or 4 chocolate curls from chocolate bar; set aside. Melt margarine and remaining chocolate in a double boiler. Pour crispy rice cereal in a large bowl; top with chocolate mixture. Mix well and press into 2, ungreased 9" pie plates. Add the ice cream over the pie crust, pressing down gently to fill pie plate. Top with shaved chocolate and freeze 2 hours or until firm. Remove pies from freezer about 15 minutes before serving. Makes 12 to 16 servings.

Some cards are just too pretty to toss after the holidays. Trim them with decorative-edge scissors and quick as a wink they become gift tags, ornaments or placecards.

Betty's Pistachio Cake

Kimberlee Schmidgall
Tremont, IL

Growing up, I remember Great Aunt Betty bringing this recipe to all family get-togethers. She always had a smile, hug and kiss for everyone...and still does today!

18-1/4 oz. pkg. white cake mix
2 3-1/2 oz. pkgs. instant
    pistachio pudding mix,
    divided
3 eggs

1 c. lemon-lime soda
1 c. oil
1 c. chopped pecans, divided
1-1/2 c. cold milk
2 c. whipped topping

Stir together cake mix, one package pudding mix, eggs, lemon-lime soda, oil and 1/2 cup pecans; beat at medium speed for 4 minutes. Pour batter into a greased and floured 13"x9" baking dish. Bake at 350 degrees for 40 minutes or until cake tests done; cool. Blend together remaining pudding mix and cold milk; beat for 2 minutes. Fold in whipped topping and spread on cake. Sprinkle on remaining pecans and refrigerate for one to 2 hours before serving. Makes 10 to 12 servings.

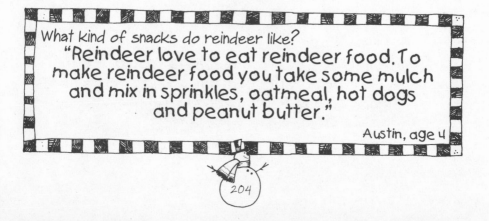

What kind of snacks do reindeer like?
"Reindeer love to eat reindeer food. To make reindeer food you take some mulch and mix in sprinkles, oatmeal, hot dogs and peanut butter."

Austin, age 4

Sweet Treats

Creamy Peach Pudding

Cathy Hughes
Cleveland, TN

Peaches and cinnamon just seem to go together.

5-1/4 oz. pkg. instant vanilla
    pudding mix
3/4 c. all-purpose flour
3/4 c. milk
15-oz. can sliced peaches,
    drained and juice reserved

8-oz. pkg. cream cheese,
    softened
3/4 c. sugar
3/4 c. powdered sugar
Garnish: cinnamon to taste

Prepare pudding mix according to package directions. Blend pudding mix and flour; stir in milk and peach juice. Pour into an 8"x8" baking dish coated with non-stick vegetable spray. Place peach slices on top of pudding mixture. Blend cream cheese, sugar and powdered sugar together and spoon on top of peaches. Sprinkle with cinnamon and bake at 350 degrees for 30 to 40 minutes. Makes 6 to 8 servings.

Christmas is not a time nor a season,
but a state of mind.

–Calvin Coolidge

Dreamy Lemon Mousse

Vicki Carver
Dayton, OH

Pretty spooned into tall glasses.

1-1/2 c. whipping cream
1/3 c. sugar
1/4 c. lemon juice

1 t. lemon extract
Garnish: lemon zest

Beat together whipping cream, sugar, lemon juice and lemon extract until thick enough to softly hold its shape. Spoon into individual serving dishes; garnish with lemon zest. Chill for 2 to 3 hours before serving. Makes 4 servings.

Crème Brûlée

Vicki Hermanson
Reno, NV

A yummy custard topped with a brown sugar glaze.

3-1/4 oz. pkg. non-instant
  vanilla pudding mix
1 pt. half-and-half

1 t. vanilla extract
4 T. brown sugar, packed

Combine pudding and half-and-half in a medium saucepan; bring to a boil over medium heat while stirring constantly. Remove from heat and add vanilla. Pour into 4 custard dishes and sprinkle with brown sugar. Place custard dishes on a baking sheet and broil 6 inches from heat source for 2 to 3 minutes or until sugar melts. Makes 4 servings.

Sweet Treats

Cranberry Cake with Butter Sauce

Alice Metzger
Langdon, ND

There's nothing like this to top off a holiday meal...so yummy.

2 c. all-purpose flour
1 c. sugar
2 t. baking powder
1/2 t. salt

2 c. cranberries
1 c. milk
3 T. butter

Whisk together flour, sugar, baking powder and salt. Add cranberries, milk and 3 tablespoons butter; mix well. Pour into a greased 8"x8" baking dish. Bake at 375 degrees for 30 minutes. Makes 6 to 8 servings.

Butter Sauce:

1/2 c. butter, melted
3/4 c. heavy cream

1 c. sugar

In a saucepan, combine butter, cream and sugar; bring to a boil for one minute. Pour butter sauce over warm cake.

How do Santa & Mrs. Claus decorate their home?
"Since Santa and his elves are busy making toys, Santa goes to the store and buys all his decorations. He puts a Christmas tree with lots of lights in every room. They also use a lot of mistletoe."

Brooke, age 8

Dutch Apple Crisp

Sophie Murphey
Castleford, ID

Top off with cinnamon ice cream for an incredible dessert.

4 c. apples, peeled and sliced
1 T. lemon juice
1/3 c. all-purpose flour
1/2 c. brown sugar, packed

1/2 t. salt
1 t. cinnamon
1/3 c. butter, melted

Place apples in a 2-quart baking dish; sprinkle with lemon juice. Combine flour, brown sugar, salt and cinnamon. Add butter and mix until crumbly; sprinkle over apples. Bake at 375 degrees for 30 minutes or until apples are tender. Makes 6 servings.

Hang cheery mittens or Santa hats on the mantel instead of stockings this year...filled with goodies and sweet treats, they're sure to be a hit!

Sweet Treats

Peanut Butter Pie

Dawn Joyce
Sciotoville, OH

You can always use a chocolate pie crust and top with chocolate curls for a peanut butter-chocolate combination everyone loves.

1/2 c. powdered sugar
1/3 c. creamy peanut butter
9-inch pie crust, baked
2-1/2 c. milk

5-1/4 oz. pkg. instant vanilla
   pudding mix
8 oz. whipped topping

Stir together powdered sugar and peanut butter, mixture will be crumbly. Spoon about 3/4 of mixture in the pie crust. In a separate mixing bowl, combine milk and vanilla pudding mix until thick; pour over peanut butter mixture. Add whipped topping and sprinkle with remaining peanut butter mixture. Makes 6 to 8 servings.

What's your favorite treat to leave Santa?
"I like to leave chocolate chip cookies because Santa always eats that kind."

Wendy, age 6

209

Gingerbread with Lemon Sauce

Kathie Williams
Oakland City, IN

There's nothing like homemade gingerbread, share
this with someone you love.

1 c. brown sugar, packed
1 c. molasses
1 c. less 1 T. shortening
2-1/2 c. all-purpose flour
1 t. ground ginger

1 t. ground cloves
1 t. cinnamon
1 c. water
1-1/2 t. baking soda
2 eggs, beaten

Beat together brown sugar, molasses and shortening; set aside. Whisk together flour and spices, then in a separate mixing bowl, combine water and baking soda. Add flour alternately with water to molasses mixture and beat until well combined. Add eggs, stirring well, and pour batter into a greased 13"x9" baking dish. Bake at 350 degrees for 30 to 45 minutes or when cake springs back to the touch. Cut cake into squares and when ready to serve, spoon on lemon sauce. Makes 10 to 12 servings.

Lemon Sauce:

1/2 c. sugar
2 T. cornstarch
1 c. water

2 T. butter
1 T. lemon zest
1 T. lemon juice

Mix sugar and cornstarch in a medium saucepan; gradually stir in water. Cook over medium heat, stirring constantly, until mixture thickens and boils. Boil and stir for one minute. Remove from heat; stir in remaining ingredients. Let cool until warm.

Tiny hands traced on paper make charming gift tags.

Sweet Treats

Frosty Lemon Cheesecake

Mary Ann Clark
Indian Springs, OH

Pretty topped with whole raspberries and curls of lemon zest.

3-oz. box lemon gelatin
1 c. boiling water
32 graham crackers, crushed
1 c. plus 2 T. sugar, divided
1/2 c. butter, melted

8-oz. pkg. cream cheese,
 softened
1 t. lemon extract
1/4 c. lemon juice
12-oz. can evaporated milk

Dissolve gelatin in boiling water; refrigerate until partially set. Combine graham cracker crumbs, 2 tablespoons sugar, and melted butter. Spread 3/4 of crumb mixture into an ungreased 13"x9" baking pan; chill. Beat cream cheese until smooth, then blend in sugar, lemon extract and lemon juice. Continue to beat until well blended and sugar is dissolved. Beat gelatin into cream cheese mixture; set aside. Pour evaporated milk into a mixing bowl and whip until stiff peaks form. Gently fold cream cheese mixture into whipped milk; blend and spread over crust. Sprinkle on remaining graham cracker crumbs and refrigerate overnight. Serves 12.

What do the reindeer and elves do after Christmas is over?

"Sleep until next Christmas."

Ryan, age 6

Christmas Cake

Trina Abraham
Colorado Springs, CO

Not everyone likes candied fruit, so try adding a cup of fresh cranberries instead...it's a great holiday treat.

1/2 c. walnuts, finely chopped
8-oz. pkg. cream cheese, softened
1 c. margarine
1-1/2 c. sugar
1-1/2 c. vanilla extract

4 eggs
2-1/4 c. all-purpose flour, divided
1-1/2 t. baking powder
1 c. candied fruit
1/2 c. chopped walnuts

Sprinkle a greased and floured Bundt® pan with finely chopped walnuts; set aside. Thoroughly blend together cream cheese, margarine, sugar and vanilla. Add eggs, one at a time, beating well after each. Stir together 2 cups flour and baking powder, gradually add to cream cheese mixture. Toss remaining flour with fruit and chopped walnuts; fold into batter and pour in prepared loaf pan. Bake at 325 degrees for one hour and 20 minutes. Cool for 5 minutes before removing from pan. Makes 12 to 14 servings.

Pour coarse salt in a shallow glass bowl and add lots of tea lights...instant sparkle.

Sweet Treats

Southern Nut Pie

Kim McGeorge
Ashley, OH

A traditional southern dessert that's very rich.

3 eggs
1 c. dark corn syrup
1/3 c. creamy peanut butter
1 t. vanilla extract

1/4 t. salt
1 c. dry-roasted, salted peanuts
9-inch pie crust, unbaked

Stir first 6 ingredients together; pour into pie crust. Bake at
400 degrees for 12 minutes. Reduce heat to 350 degrees and bake an
additional 30 minutes or until center is set. Makes 6 to 8 servings.

Gourmet Fruit Delight

Margaret Scoresby
Mount Vernon, OH

*On special occasions, like Christmas, we enjoy this yummy fruit
dish. It's easy to prepare and beautiful when served.*

16-oz. can pears, undrained
10-oz. bag frozen raspberries
11-oz. can mandarin oranges,
    drained
2 to 3 bananas, sliced

1 grapefruit, sectioned and
    chopped
1 c. sour cream
1/4 c. brown sugar, packed

Purée pears in blender until smooth. Pour into a large serving bowl
and fold in raspberries, oranges, bananas and grapefruit; chill one
hour. Blend together sour cream and brown sugar; spoon over
individual servings. Makes 6 to 8 servings.

Snow ice cream is always a wintertime treat, so why not
invite friends over for an ice cream party?
Everyone brings their favorite topping to
share...a great way to catch up.

213

Figgy Pudding with Custard Sauce

Mel Wolk
St. Peters, MO

Try adding dried cranberries for a slightly tart flavor.

1/2 c. butter
1/2 c. shortening
1 c. sugar
3 eggs, separated
1 c. milk
2 T. rum extract
1 apple, cored and finely
    chopped
1 lb. dried figs, finely chopped

zest of 1 lemon
zest of 1 orange
1 c. chopped pecans
1/2 t. cinnamon
1/4 t. ground cloves
1/4 t. ground ginger
1-1/2 c. bread crumbs
2 t. baking powder

Cream together butter and shortening; gradually add sugar, egg yolks, milk, rum extract, apple, figs, lemon and orange zest. Stir in pecans, cinnamon, cloves, ginger, bread crumbs and baking powder. Beat egg whites until stiff; gently fold in fig mixture. Pour into a greased Bundt® pan. Cover with a double thickness of foil. Set in a large shallow pan and place on the middle rack in oven. Fill the shallow pan half full with boiling water and steam pudding at 325 degrees for 4 hours, replacing water as needed. Serve pudding warm with custard sauce. Makes 12 servings.

Custard Sauce:

1 egg
3/4 c. sugar
1 T. water
1 t. vanilla extract

1 T. all-purpose flour
2 c. milk, scalded
1 T. butter

Combine egg, sugar, water, vanilla extract and flour; add to cooled milk. Cook over low heat until thickened. Remove from heat and stir in butter, mixing well.

214

Sweet Treats

Gram's Gooey Butter Cake

Denise Allis
Gig Harbor, WA

Yummy served warm or cold.

1/2 c. butter
4 eggs, divided
18-1/4 oz. yellow cake mix

8-oz. pkg. cream cheese,
  softened
1 lb. powdered sugar, divided

Blend together butter and 2 eggs; stir in cake mix; press into a greased 13"x9" baking dish. Combine cream cheese, remaining eggs and all but 1/4 cup powdered sugar; pour over crust. Bake at 350 degrees for 30 minutes; top with remaining 1/4 cup powdered sugar. Makes 8 to 10 servings.

How does Santa leave presents if you don't have a chimney?
"The grown-ups leave the front door open and then lock it when he leaves."

Austin, age 7

Aunt Ethel's Pound Cake

*Brenda Burkett
Williamsport, MD*

*Each time we visited Aunt Ethel she made this pound cake.
It's always been my favorite and now, when I make it,
I still see her smile and hear her laughter.*

1 c. butter
3 c. sugar
6 eggs
1/2 c. shortening

3 c. all-purpose flour
1 t. baking powder
1 c. milk
1 t. vanilla extract

Cream butter; gradually add sugar. Beat together until light and fluffy.
Add eggs, one at a time; mix in shortening. Sift flour and baking
powder together; stir in milk and vanilla. Pour batter into a greased
and floured Bundt® pan. Bake at 350 degrees for 1-1/2 hours or until
center tests done. Serves 10 to 12.

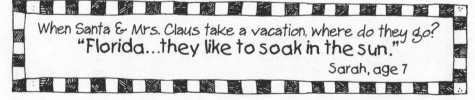

When Santa & Mrs. Claus take a vacation, where do they go?
"Florida...they like to soak in the sun."
Sarah, age 7

Sweet Treats

Bread Pudding Apple Pie

Cora Baker
La Rue, OH

*Wintertime comfort food...old-fashioned bread pudding,
brown sugar, cinnamon and golden apples.*

3 eggs, beaten
1 c. applesauce
1/2 c. vanilla yogurt
1/2 c. sugar
3/4 c. brown sugar, packed and
   divided
1/2 c. long-cooking oats,
   uncooked

1 t. cinnamon
3 c. bread, cubed
2 apples, peeled, cored and
   chopped
9-inch pie crust, unbaked
1/4 c. all-purpose flour
2 T. butter

Stir together eggs, applesauce, yogurt, sugar, 1/2 cup brown sugar,
oats and cinnamon. Add bread and apples; spoon mixture in pie crust.
Blend together remaining brown sugar and flour; cut in butter until
mixture resembles coarse crumbs; sprinkle over pie filling. Bake at
350 degrees for one hour or until top is golden and fruit is tender.
Makes 8 servings.

For Christmas is tradition time...traditions that recall the
precious memories down the years.

-Helen Lowrie Marshall

217

S'more Fun

Everyone loves sweets...it's one of the best parts of the holidays! This year, gather friends, neighbors and family for a dessert party.

Be sure to deliver your invitations early in December and make them festive and fun...pipe frosting on a large gingerbread cookie, use a gold glitter pen on a glass ornament or trim colorful paper with decorative-edge scissors and jot down the words to your favorite holiday song on the front.

Pull out your cookbooks and choose a variety of cakes, cookies, candy, pastries, pies and brownies, then narrow your list down to those you like best. Look for recipes that can be made ahead of time and frozen to save time.

Fill cake plates with cookies, cut gingerbread in star shapes, bake and layer them around the base of your punch bowl for an edible cookie ring. Slide gumdrops, peppermints and mints on wax-covered string then wind it around your buffet table or use as garland for your tree. Don't forget to serve lots of creamy cocoa, coffee, eggnog and spiced cider, too.

Index

Index

Index

We've cooked up a whole collection of Gooseberry Patch® books!

Have a taste for more? Call us toll-free at
1-800-854-6673

We'll send you our latest catalog filled with snowmen, Santas, ornaments, candles, cookie cutters, gourmet goodies, calendars, giftwrap, pottery, collectibles and MORE...including our best-selling cookbooks!

Phone us:
1·800·854·6673

Fax us:
1·740·363·7225

Visit our website:
gooseberrypatch.com

Send us your favorite recipe!

and the memory that makes it special for you!* If we select your recipe for a brand new **Gooseberry Patch** cookbook, your name will appear right along with it...and you'll receive a FREE copy of the book! Mail to:

Vickie & Jo Ann
Gooseberry Patch, Dept. BOOK
P.O. Box 190
Delaware, Ohio 43015

*Please include the number of servings and all other necessary information!

SNOW ANGELS ❄ SPARKLY SNOWFLAKES ❄ ROSY CHEEKS ❄ SWEET DREAMS ❄ FROSTY WINDOWS ❄ GOOEY S'MORES ❄ LAUGHTER ❄ JOLLY HOLIDAYS ❄ SUGAR PLUMS ❄ GIGGLES ❄ SNUGGLED IN ❄ SNOW GLOBES ❄ WINTER WONDERLAND ❄ I BELIEVE ❄ GUMDROPS ❄ SPARKLES & WISHES ❄

SNOW ANGELS ✳ SPARKLY SNOWFLAKES ✳ ROSY CHE... EKS ✳ SWEET DREAMS ✳ FROSTY WINDOWS ✳ GOOEY S'MORES ✳ LAUGHTER ✳ JOLLY HOLIDAYS ✳ SUGAR PLUMS ✳ GIGGLES ✳ SNUGGLED IN ✳ SNO... OW GLOBES ✳ WINTER WONDERLAND ✳ I BELIEVE ✳ GUMDROPS ✳ SPARKLES & WISHES